HARCOURT

Science

Harcourt School Publishers

Orlando • Boston • Dallas • Chicago • San Diego

www.harcourtschool.com

Cover Image
This is a Bengal tiger cub. The
Bengal tiger is a native of India
and is an endangered animal.

ISBN 0-15-317497-8

6 7 8 9 10 032 2002 2001 2000

Authors

Marjorie Slavick Frank
Former Adjunct Faculty Member at
    Hunter, Brooklyn, and Manhattan
    Colleges
New York, New York

Robert M. Jones
Professor of Education
University of Houston-Clear Lake
Houston, Texas

Gerald H. Krockover
Professor of Earth and Atmospheric
    Science Education
School Mathematics and Science
    Center
Purdue University
West Lafayette, Indiana

Mozell P. Lang
Science Education Consultant
Michigan Department of Education
Lansing, Michigan

Joyce C. McLeod
Visiting Professor
Rollins College
Winter Park, Florida

Carol J. Valenta
Vice President—Education, Exhibits,
    and Programs
St. Louis Science Center
St. Louis, Missouri

Barry A. Van Deman
Science Program Director
Arlington, Virginia

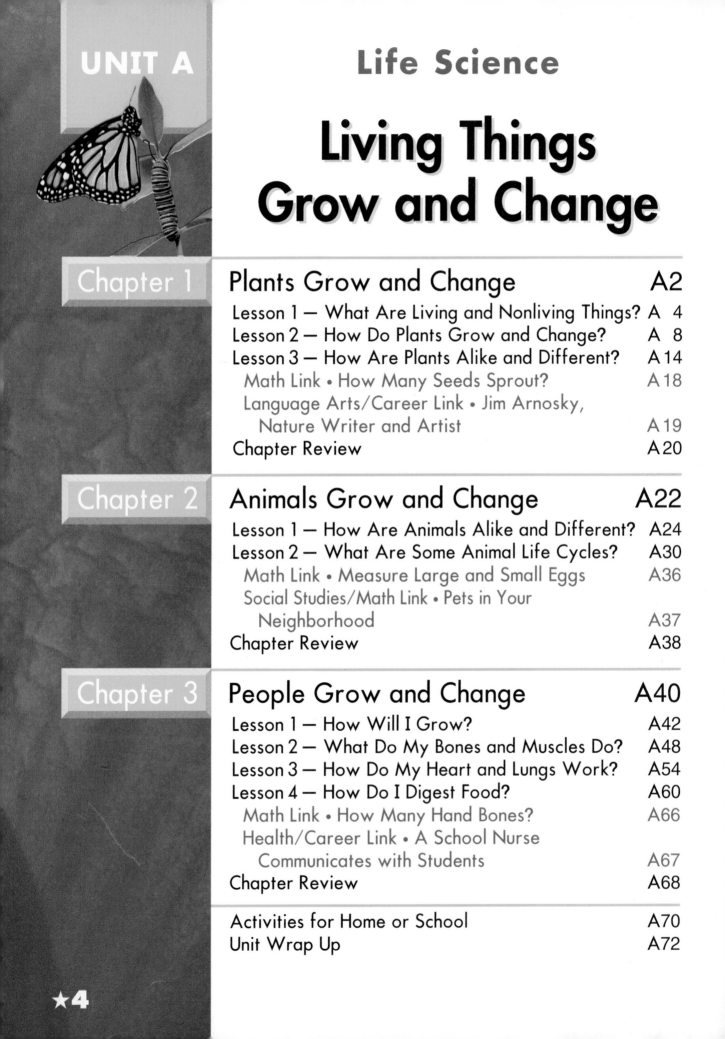

Life Science

Living Things Grow and Change

Life Science

Homes for Living Things

UNIT C

Earth Science

Exploring Earth's Surface

UNIT D

Earth Science

Space and Weather

Physical Science

Exploring Matter

Physical Science

Energy in Motion

Using Science Skills

Observe.

Use your five senses to help you learn.

Compare.

Tell how things are alike and different.

Sequence.

Put things in time order to show changes.

Classify.

Sort objects into groups to show how they are alike.

Infer.

Use what you know to make a good guess about why something is happening.

Gather information.

Use computers, books, and what you observe.

Plan.

Decide step by step how to investigate your ideas.

Make models.

Make something to show what a thing is like or how it works.

Measure.

Use tools to find out
how far or how much.

Predict.

Use what you know
to make a good
guess about what
will happen.

Draw conclusions.

Use all the information you have gathered to make decisions.

Communicate.

Share what you know by telling or showing others.

Science Safety

Think ahead.

Be neat.

Be careful.

Do not eat or drink things.

Safety Symbols

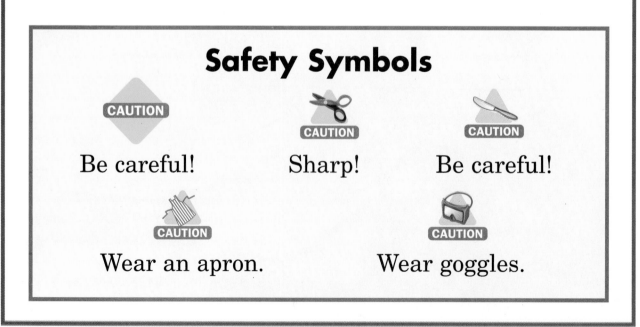

CAUTION

Be careful!

CAUTION

Sharp!

CAUTION

Be careful!

CAUTION

Wear an apron.

CAUTION

Wear goggles.

Living Things Grow and Change

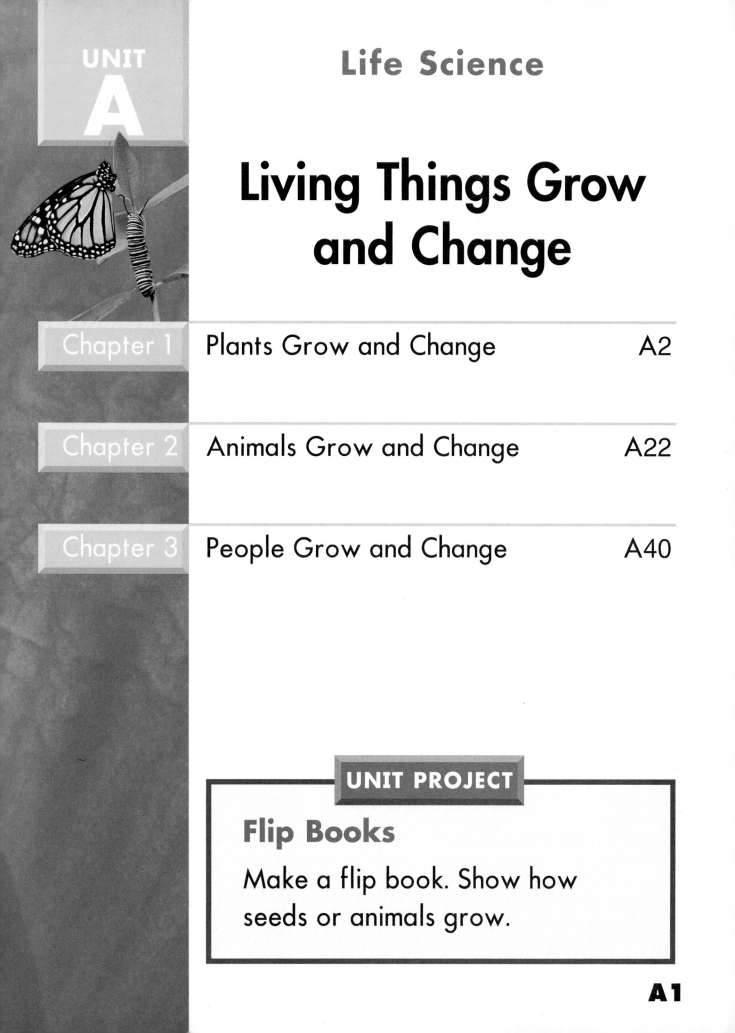

UNIT
A

Life Science

Living Things Grow and Change

UNIT PROJECT

Flip Books

Make a flip book. Show how seeds or animals grow.

Plants Grow and Change

living
nonliving
nutrients
seed coat
germinate
seedling
cactus

Did You Know?
The redwood tree is the tallest living thing in the United States.

Did You Know?

The part of popcorn that sticks between your teeth is the **seed coat**.

What Are Living and Nonliving Things?

Living and Nonliving Things

You will need

picture cards

paper and pencil

What Am I?	
Living	Nonliving

① Make a chart like the one above.

② Look at each picture card. Does it show a living thing or a nonliving thing?

③ Record in your chart.

④ Compare the things in the chart.

Science Skill

When you compare things, you tell how they are alike and different.

Living and Nonliving Things

The world is made up of living things and nonliving things. All **living** things grow and change. They need food, water, and air. Things that are not alive are **nonliving**. They do not need food, water, and air.

nonliving things

living things

Living Things Grow and Change

A tree and a chick are living things. They come from other living things. Like all living things, they need food, air, and water. Like all living things, they grow and change.

■ **How do you think the chick will change?**

Living Things Need Nonliving Things

Air, water, and light are nonliving things. They do not grow. They do not need food.

Living things need nonliving things. Plants need air, water, and light to grow. People and animals need air, food, and water to live.

■ **What nonliving thing is this girl drinking?**

Think About It

1. What are three ways living things are alike?
2. How do living things use nonliving things?

How Do Plants Grow and Change?

What Plants Need

You will need

2 plants

cup of water

paper and pencil

What Happens to a Plant	
Plant with Water	Plant with No Water

1 Make a chart like the one above.

2 Put both plants in a sunny place. Water the soil of only one plant. Predict what will happen.

3 Observe both plants every day. Write the date. Record any changes.

Science Skill

When you observe the plants, use your senses of sight, touch, smell, and hearing.

What the Parts of a Plant Do

A plant needs light, air, and water to grow. It also needs **nutrients**, or minerals, from soil. Each part of a plant helps the plant get what it needs. When a plant gets what it needs, it can grow and change.

Flowers make seeds.

Leaves use light, air, water, and nutrients to make food for the plant.

Stems hold up the plant and move water and nutrients through it.

Roots take in water and nutrients from the soil.

How Plants Grow from Seeds

Seeds have different parts. Most seeds have a covering called a **seed coat**, which protects the seed. The seed is made up of stored food and a tiny plant. The tiny plant uses the stored food when it begins to grow.

When a seed gets water and warmth, it may **germinate**, or start to grow. First the roots grow down. Then a stem grows up. The young plant is called a **seedling**.

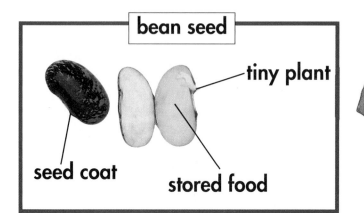

bean seed

tiny plant

seed coat

stored food

seedling, 4 days

seedling, 15 days

As the seedling grows, it changes. It makes more leaves and stems. The stems get taller and thicker. When the plant is full grown, its flowers make seeds. Then the pattern of growing and changing starts again.

plant, 45 days

adult plant with seeds

Plants Can Change

If plants do not get what they need, they may not grow. The rain, sunlight, and even insects in a place can make the plants change. If a field does not get rain for a long time, the plants there will not get the water they need.

■ **How can you tell that these plants did not get the water they needed?**

A plant needs light from all sides. If it gets light from just one side, its stems and leaves grow toward the light. This helps the plant get the light it needs to make food and grow.

■ **Why does this plant grow toward the light?**

Insects may eat the leaves of a plant. Without leaves, the plant cannot make the food it needs. It may die.

Think About It

1. What happens when a seed germinates?
2. What are some ways plants may change?

How Are Plants Alike and Different?

How to Classify Leaves

You will need

leaves

index cards and pencil

1 Observe the leaves. Look for ways they are alike.

2 Classify the leaves into groups. Leaves in each group should be alike in some way.

3 Write a label for each group that tells how the leaves are alike. Tell about the leaves where you live.

Science Skill

When you classify things, you sort them into groups that show how they are alike.

Plants in Different Places

Plants live in almost every part of the world. Different kinds of plants grow in different places.

pine forest

oak forest

desert

How Plants Are Different

A pine tree has leaves that look like needles. Its small, hard seeds grow in cones. The outside of the cone protects the seeds until they are ready to germinate.

An oak tree has leaves that are broad and flat. Oak trees grow from seeds called acorns.

pine cone

pine seeds

acorns

■ How is an acorn different from a pine cone?

cactus flower

A **cactus** plant can store water in its thick stems. Its leaves are sharp spines. The spines protect the stems from animals that might eat them.

Cactuses also grow flowers. Like all flowers, cactus flowers grow into fruits. The cactus seeds are inside the fruits.

Think About It

1. What are some places plants live?
2. How are plants in different places alike and different?

Math Link

How Many Seeds Sprout?

Hundreds of walnuts grow on this walnut tree. A new tree could grow from each walnut. Most of the walnuts will not germinate. Animals will eat some of them. Others will not get the things they need to grow.

Think and Do

Count and record the number of seeds in an orange. Then plant the seeds. Make sure they have water and warmth. Count and record the number of seeds that germinate and grow. Write a subtraction sentence that tells how many seeds did not grow.

Jim Arnosky, Nature Writer and Artist

Jim Arnosky first worked as a naturalist. A naturalist studies plants and animals in the wild. Now he writes and illustrates children's books. In some of Jim Arnosky's books, the character Crinkleroot helps children learn about living things in nature.

Think and Do

Draw your own character. Use your character in a story about living things. Share your story.

REVIEW

Tell What You Know

1. How are these plants alike and different?

2. How are the plants different from nonliving things?

3. How did these plants grow from seeds?

Vocabulary

Tell the term that completes the sentence.

> **seedling**   **germinate**   **nutrients**
> **living thing**   **nonliving thing**

4. Plants need water and warmth to _____ .

5. A _____ does not need food, water, and air.

6. A _____ is a young plant.

7. Plants need _____ , or minerals, from the soil.

8. A _____ grows and changes.

Using Science Skills

9. **Observe and Compare** Make a chart like this one to record what you observe about seeds. Tape seeds from different plants onto the chart. Tell what plant each seed comes from. Write your observations in the chart. Compare your observations with those of a classmate.

What I Observe About Seeds		
Seed	Plant	Observations

10. **Classify** Sort things in your classroom into groups of living things and nonliving things. List the things in each group. Tell why you put each thing in the group you did.

CHAPTER 2

Animals Grow and Change

mammal
reptile
amphibian
insect
life cycle

Did You Know?

The largest **mammal** in the world is the blue whale.

Did You Know? The walking stick is the longest **insect** in the world. It is 13 inches long.

How Are Animals Alike and Different?

Ways to Group Animals

You will need

animal
picture cards

index cards and pencil

1 Observe the animals to see how they are alike and different.

2 Classify the animals into groups. Animals in a group should be alike somehow.

3 Write a label for each group that tells how the animals are alike.

Science Skill

When you classify animals, you put them into groups to show how the animals are alike.

Many Kinds of Animals

Some animals have fur. Others have feathers or scales. Some animals use special body parts to fly, swim, or walk.

giraffe

tree cricket

alligator

puffin

clown fish

Animals With Bones

Animals can be grouped by their body parts. All the animals on these two pages have bones inside their bodies. They have other body parts that make them different.

Cats and dogs are mammals. A **mammal** is an animal that has fur or hair. A mother mammal makes milk and feeds it to its young.

Birds have feathers to protect their bodies. They also have wings. Most birds use their wings to fly.

blue jay

chameleon

Lizards, snakes, and turtles are reptiles. A **reptile** is an animal that is covered with scales. Its skin is rough and dry.

Frogs and toads are amphibians. An **amphibian** often has smooth, wet skin. Its skin helps it live both in water and on land.

All fish live in water. A fish uses its fins to swim and its gills to breathe.

■ **What tells you that these animals are not mammals?**

leaf frog

fish

Animals Without Bones

The animals on these two pages have no bones. They have other body parts that make them different.

Praying mantises, ants, and bees are insects. An **insect** is an animal that has three body parts and six legs. Many insects also have four wings. Spiders are not insects. They have eight legs.

praying mantis

golden silk spider

Worms have soft bodies. They do not use legs to walk. Instead, worms use their bodies to crawl.

Like a worm, a snail has a soft body that it uses to move. It may also have a hard shell to protect it.

snail

earthworm

■ **How are the worm and the snail alike and different?**

Think About It

1. What are some ways animals are alike? How are they different?
2. How can animals be grouped by their body parts?

What Are Some Animal Life Cycles?

Investigate

How Mealworms Grow and Change

You will need

mealworms

mealworm home with meal

bottle cap with water

hand lens

1 Feed your mealworms. Give them water each day.

2 Observe the mealworms every day with the hand lens.

3 Each day draw a picture of what you observe. Write the date and a sentence about changes you see.

Science Skill

You can use a hand lens to help you observe details.

How Animals Grow and Change

These goslings and the lion cub are still young. They will keep growing and changing. They will grow up to look like their parents. Together, all the parts of an animal's life from birth to death make up its **life cycle**.

Canada geese

goslings

African lions

cub

How Birds Grow and Change

Birds lay eggs. First, a mother bird lays her eggs in a nest. Next, the mother or father sits on the eggs to keep them warm.

unhatched eggs in nest

A chick grows inside each egg until it gets too big for it. Then the chick breaks the eggshell and hatches.

As the chicks grow and change, they get new feathers. They will grow up to look like their parents.

Life Cycle of a Robin

adult bird

Most bird parents take care of their chicks. The parents feed and protect them until they can take care of themselves. Soon after the birds are grown, they can have chicks of their own.

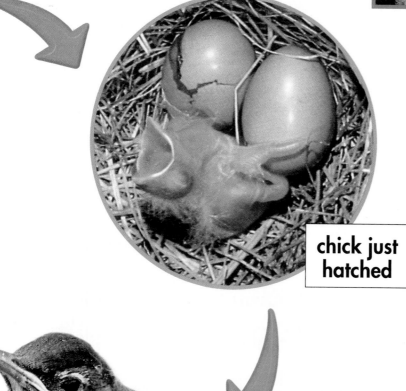

chick just hatched

chick almost ready to fly

How Mammals Grow and Change

All young mammals start growing inside their mothers' bodies. The adult cat here has kittens growing inside her. When they are big enough, the kittens will be born.

Life Cycle of a Cat

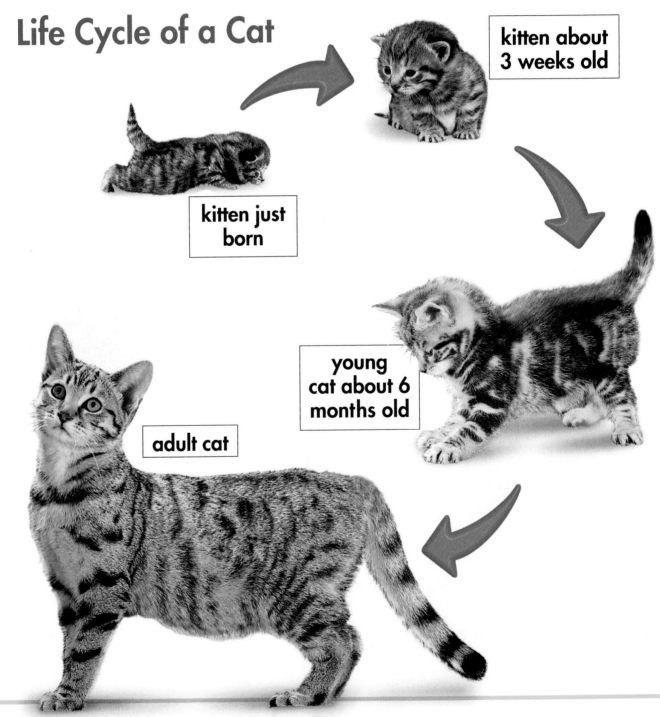

kitten about 3 weeks old

kitten just born

young cat about 6 months old

adult cat

Like all young mammals, these kittens drink milk from their mother. The milk helps the kittens grow bigger and stronger. By the time they are one year old, they are full grown.

■ **How do the kittens look like their mother? How do they look different?**

Think About It

1. How do young animals change as they grow into adults?
2. What do young animals grow to look like?

A veterinarian is a doctor who cares for animals. This cat is going to have kittens. Why do you think the veterinarian is checking her?

Math Link

Measure Large and Small Eggs

The ostrich lays the biggest eggs. The hummingbird lays the smallest eggs. Compare the sizes of the eggs to the size of a chicken egg.

ostrich egg

chicken egg

hummingbird egg

Think and Do

The photographs show the real sizes of eggs from different birds. Use a ruler to measure the picture of each egg. Make a chart and list the kinds of eggs in order from biggest to smallest. Beside each name, write how long the egg is.

Pets in Your Neighborhood

People keep many kinds of animals as pets. In many neighborhoods, people have dogs and cats. Dogs and cats are mammals. Some people have reptiles, fish, and birds.

Think and Do

Talk to classmates or neighbors who have pets. Think about the animal group each pet belongs to. Show what you find out in a bar graph. Use the graph to talk about which animal groups most of the pets belong to.

Pets

Mammal	🐾	🐾	🐾	🐾	
Bird	🐾	🐾			
Reptile	🐾				
Amphibian	🐾				
Fish	🐾	🐾			

Tell What You Know

1. How are these animals alike?

2. How are the animals different?

3. What is the life cycle of each animal?

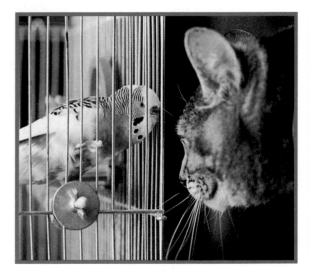

Vocabulary

Tell the term that completes the sentence.

amphibian	reptile	mammal
insect	life cycle	

4. An _____ has six legs.

5. A _____ has scales that are rough and dry.

6. A _____ has fur or hair.

7. A _____ is the way an animal grows and changes.

8. An _____ has smooth, wet skin.

Using Science Skills

9. **Classify** Go for a walk outside with your class. Look for different kinds of animals. Write down the name of each one you see. What animal group does it belong to? Write the group name next to the animal name. Then tell a classmate how you know what animal group each one belongs to.

Animal	Kind
robin	bird
Squirrel	mammal
bee	insect

10. **Observe** These pictures show the life cycle of a butterfly. Observe the changes from one picture to the next. Think about what you know about animal life cycles. Then use the pictures to tell what happens in a butterfly's life cycle.

People Grow and Change

Vocabulary

permanent
teeth

skeleton

muscles

heart

lungs

heart rate

digest

saliva

stomach

Did You Know?
Your heart beats
more than 66 times
a minute.

Did You Know?

It takes 43 **muscles** to frown but only 17 muscles to smile.

How Will I Grow?

Investigate

How Hands Grow and Change

You will need

paper and pencil

1 Trace your hand on the left side of your paper.

2 Predict what your hand will look like when you grow up. Draw a picture of it.

3 Compare the two hands. Tell how they are alike and different.

Science Skill

When you predict, you use what you know to make a good guess about what will happen.

How Your Body Grows and Changes

Your body grows and changes in many ways. You get bigger and taller. You get stronger and heavier. How has the boy in these pictures grown and changed?

Joey, 8 years old

Joey, 4 years old

Joey, 4 months old

A43

All People Grow and Change

All people grow and change. You are growing and changing. First, you were a baby. Now, you are a child. Later on, you will be a teenager. After that, you will become an adult.

■ **Predict how the three children in this family will grow and change.**

son
8 months

daughter
7 years

son
15 years

When you are an adult, you will change in other ways. As you get older, your hair may turn gray or white. Your skin will get wrinkles.

mother
37 years

father
42 years

grandmother
65 years

A45

Growing in Other Ways

Growing is more than getting bigger. You also change in other ways as you grow. When you were a baby, your first teeth grew in. Now you are losing those teeth. New adult teeth, called **permanent teeth**, are growing in to take their place.

Learning is another way you grow and change. You are changing as you learn new things.

Some things you learn can also help you exercise. Exercise such as dancing helps your body grow strong and stay healthy.

■ **How is this girl helping her body? What is she learning?**

Think About It

1. How do people grow and change?
2. How can you help yourself grow and change?

What Do My Bones and Muscles Do?

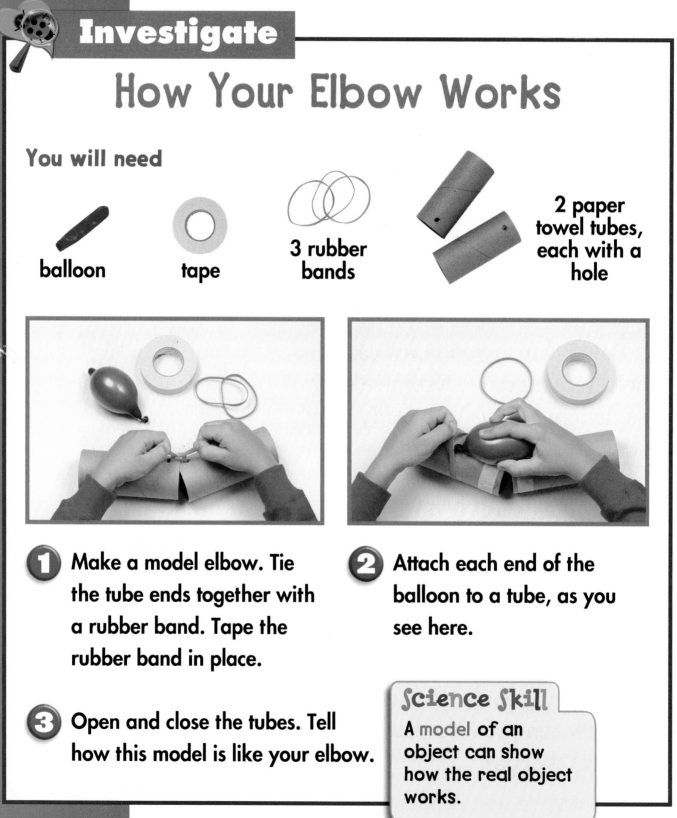

Investigate

How Your Elbow Works

You will need

balloon

tape

3 rubber bands

2 paper towel tubes, each with a hole

1 Make a model elbow. Tie the tube ends together with a rubber band. Tape the rubber band in place.

2 Attach each end of the balloon to a tube, as you see here.

3 Open and close the tubes. Tell how this model is like your elbow.

Science Skill

A model of an object can show how the real object works.

Your Bones and Muscles

Under your skin are hundreds of bones and muscles. Your bones and muscles work together. They help you sit, stand, walk, run, and move in many other ways.

muscles

bones

What Your Bones Do

Your bones fit together to make your **skeleton**. Your skeleton holds up your body and gives it shape.

Some bones help you move. Other bones protect parts inside your body. Your ribs protect your heart and lungs. Your skull protects your brain.

■ **Which bones help you move?**

arm bones

hand bones

skull

ribs

spine, or backbone

hip bones

leg bones

foot bones

What Your Muscles Do

Your **muscles** are body parts that work to move your bones and do other jobs. Your heart is a muscle that pumps blood through your body.

arm muscles

shoulder muscles

stomach muscles

chest muscles

leg muscles

■ What muscles is the boy using to move?

Your Bones and Muscles Work Together

Muscles work in pairs to move your bones. One muscle pulls a bone to move it. Then the other muscle pulls the bone to move it back.

■ **How do this boy's muscles move his leg bones?**

Keeping Bones and Muscles Healthy

You can keep your bones and muscles strong and healthy. Exercising every day helps your bones and muscles stay strong. Eating healthful food keeps them healthy.

■ How are these children keeping their bones and muscles strong and healthy?

Think About It

1. How do your bones and muscles work together?
2. How can you keep your bones and muscles strong and healthy?

How Do My Heart and Lungs Work?

Investigate

A Heartbeat

You will need

paper cup
with bottom cut out

1 Work with a partner. Your partner will use the cup to listen to your heartbeat.

2 Jump up and down while your partner counts to 10.

3 Your partner will observe your heartbeat again. Is it faster or slower? Trade places.

Science Skill

When you observe, you may use tools along with your senses.

Your Heart and Lungs

Your heart and lungs help keep you alive. Your **heart** is a muscle that pumps blood to every part of your body. Your **lungs** are body parts that help you breathe the air you need to live.

■ How can you tell that your heart and lungs work harder when you exercise?

A55

How Your Heart Works

Your heart is about the size of your fist. Each time your heart beats, it pumps blood to all the parts of your body.

Your **heart rate** is how fast or slowly your heart beats. When you exercise, your heart beats faster. Your heart rate is faster. When you rest, your heart rate is slower.

■ **In what part of your body is your heart?**

How Your Lungs Work

You have two lungs inside your chest. Air goes in and out of your lungs when you breathe. When you breathe in, the air moves down a tube into your lungs. Your lungs fill with air and get larger. When you breathe out, air leaves your lungs.

■ **Compare the inside and outside of a lung. How are they different?**

Your Heart and Lungs Work Together

Your heart and lungs work together to get your body the oxygen it needs. Your heart pumps blood first to your lungs. Your lungs take in oxygen from the air you breathe. The blood picks up the oxygen and takes it back to your heart. Then your heart pumps the blood to all parts of your body.

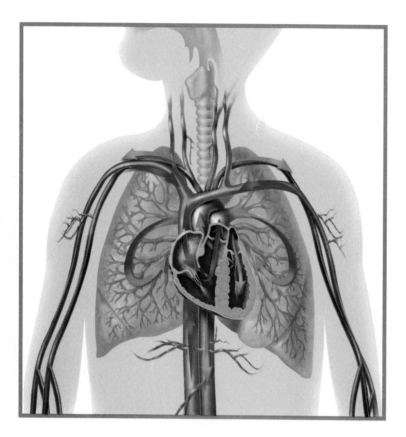

■ How does blood get to your lungs? Where does it go after that?

When the blood comes back to your heart, it is pumped to your lungs again for more oxygen.

■ **How is this boy keeping his heart and lungs healthy?**

Keeping Your Heart and Lungs Healthy

It is important to keep your heart and lungs healthy. Exercise helps your heart and lungs as well as your bones and muscles. When you exercise, your heart and lungs work harder and get stronger.

Think About It

1. How do your heart and lungs work together?
2. How can you keep your heart and lungs healthy?

How Do I Digest Food?

How Digestion Begins

You will need

cracker   mirror   paper and pencil

1 Observe the cracker. Draw it.

2 Put the cracker in your mouth. Do not chew it. Count slowly to 20.

3 Think about how the cracker feels. Use the mirror to observe it.

4 Draw what you observe. Tell what you think is happening.

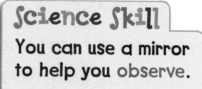

Science Skill
You can use a mirror to help you observe.

How Your Body Digests Food

Healthful food has the energy and nutrients your body needs to grow and stay healthy. To get the energy and nutrients, your body must **digest**, or break down, the food.

mouth

tube to the stomach

stomach

small intestine

large intestine

A61

How Your Body Digests Food

Your body starts to digest food in your mouth. When you chew your food, it mixes with saliva. **Saliva** is the liquid in your mouth that begins to break down food.

When you swallow the food you have chewed, it goes down a tube. Muscles in the tube push the food to your stomach.

mouth

tube to the stomach

■ **Where does your body start to digest food?**

Your **stomach** is like a bag made of muscles. The muscles squeeze the food and mix it with special juices. The food turns into a thick liquid.

The liquid food moves into your small intestine. From there, the nutrients from the food go into your blood. Your blood carries the nutrients to all parts of your body. Food parts that your body does not need move into your large intestine.

mouth

tube to the stomach

stomach

small intestine

large intestine

Eating Healthful Foods

Healthful foods keep you healthy. They help your body grow and give you energy. Eating just one kind of food will not give your body everything it needs. You should eat different kinds of foods every day.

The Food Guide Pyramid can help you choose healthful foods. You need foods from each group. The foods you should eat the most of are at the bottom. The foods you should eat the least of are at the top.

■ **What healthful foods are the boy and his mother eating?**

fats, oils, sweets

milk, yogurt, cheese

meat, poultry, fish, dry beans, eggs, nuts

vegetables

fruits

bread, cereal, rice, pasta

Think About It

1. How does your body digest food?
2. What are some healthful foods?

Math Link

How Many Hand Bones?

Your wrist, palm, and fingers are all parts of your hand. Each part has many bones. You can see them in this picture. There are 8 bones in your wrist and 5 bones in your palm. There are 14 bones in your fingers.

hand X ray

Think and Do

Trace your hand. Then draw in the bones. Write an addition problem to show how many bones there are in all.

A66

A School Nurse Communicates with Students

School nurses and health aides help keep you healthy. This nurse is checking to see that this boy is growing well. A nurse also checks weight and height. He or she may take care of you when you are ill.

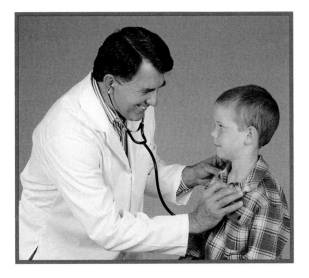

Think and Do

Write some questions you would like to ask a school nurse about keeping healthy. Invite your school nurse or health aide to visit your class. Get answers to your questions.

Tell What You Know

1. Use the pictures to tell how people grow and change.

Vocabulary

Use the terms in the box to tell about each picture.

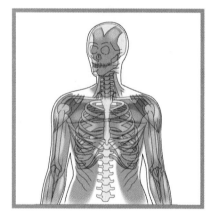

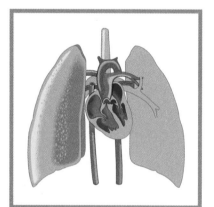

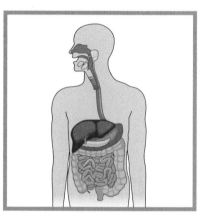

2. permanent teeth

   skeleton

   muscles

3. heart

   heart rate

   lungs

4. digest

   saliva

   stomach

Using Science Skills

5. Observe For two days, observe what you do to be healthy. Make a list of your observations. Then use your list to talk about how you help yourself be healthy.

6. Compare Look at a baby picture of yourself. Then make a chart like this one. How are you the same and different now?

Me		
	As a Baby	Now
Hair Color		
Eye Color		
Teeth		
Other Things		

Grow a Sweet Potato

1. Stick toothpicks into a sweet potato. Place the sweet potato in a jar of water.

2. Put the jar in a sunny place.

3. Observe the sweet potato for a month.

4. Draw pictures to show how the sweet potato grows and changes.

Go on an Animal Search

1. Look through magazines and books for pictures of animals.

2. List the names of the animals.

3. Group the animals. Make a chart to show your groups and tell how many of each kind you found.

4. Share your chart and list with classmates.

Animals
robins
sparrow
frog
collie
poodle

Animal Group	How Many
fish	
reptiles	
amphibians	
birds	//
mammals	

Measure Shoe Lengths

1. Trace your shoe and the shoe of an adult.

2. Measure how long each drawing is. Write the two measurements.

3. Subtract to find the difference between the two.

4. Infer what happens to children's feet over time.

Observe a Plant Without Leaves

1. Take all the leaves off a small plant.

2. Set the plant in a sunny place, and keep the plant watered.

3. Predict what will happen.

4. Observe the plant every day.

5. Draw pictures to show what happens.

Wrap Up

WRITING
Sequence Game
Choose a plant or an animal. Draw and write about how it grows. Put one or more of your steps behind a flap for classmates to guess.

READING
Big Blue Whale
by Nicola Davies
How does the largest mammal on Earth grow and change? Read this book to find out.

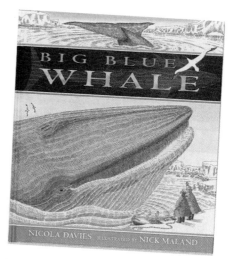

COMPUTER CENTER
Visit *The Learning Site* at
www.harcourtschool.com

Homes for Living Things

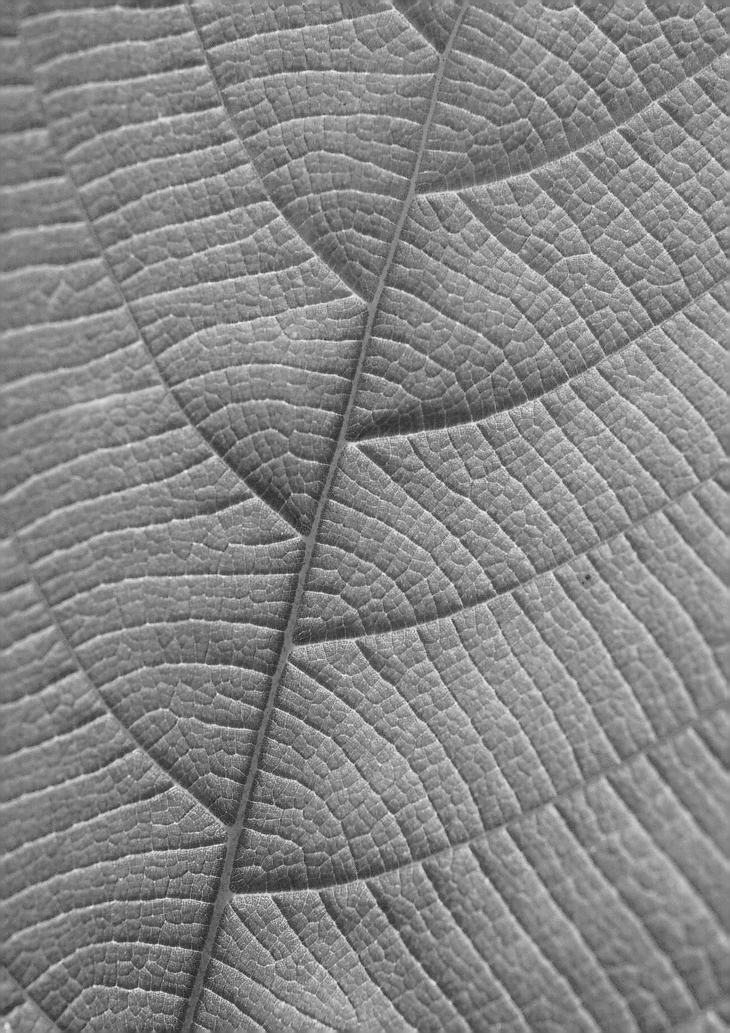

Life Science

Homes for Living Things

UNIT PROJECT

It's a Small World

Make forest and desert terrariums. Find out about soils and plants you will need.

Habitats for Plants and Animals

Vocabulary

environment

habitat

desert

rain forest

woodland forest

Arctic

pond

food chain

Did You Know?

About half of all the kinds of plants and animals on Earth live in the **rain forest**.

Did You Know?

The Sahara, a **desert** in Africa, is about as big as the whole United States.

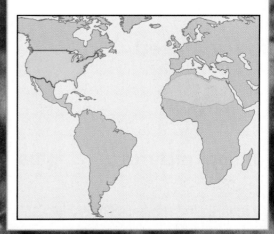

What Is a Habitat?

Investigate

Where Animals Can Meet Their Needs

You will need

animal pictures

glue

crayons

paper and pencil

1 Choose an animal picture. Glue it in the middle of your paper.

2 On another sheet of paper, make a list of your animal's needs.

3 Draw the things your animal needs. Use your picture to communicate your ideas.

Science Skill

When you communicate your ideas, you tell or show others what you know.

Where Animals Live

Animals live in different environments around the world. An **environment** is made up of all the living and nonliving things in a place. These caribou live in a cold environment.

Alaska

Animal Habitats

Every animal has a habitat. A **habitat** is a place where an animal finds the food and water it needs to live. An animal also finds shelter there to be safe from other animals.

An environment may have many different habitats. In a forest environment, part of the forest may be the habitat of a bear. One tree in the forest may be the habitat of a wasp.

paper wasp

Alaska brown bear

■ **How are these animals meeting their needs in their habitats?**

cougar

Animals find habitats where they can meet their needs. A pelican eats fish, so it lives by the ocean. It can easily find fish there.

grebe

sea otter

■ How are these animals meeting their needs in their water habitats?

pelican

Think About It

1. What is a habitat?
2. Why do different animals have different habitats?

What Are Different Land Habitats?

Investigate

Different Animal Habitats

You will need

animal picture cards

habitat picture cards

1 Classify the cards. Put the animal cards in one group and the habitat cards in another.

2 Observe the pictures carefully. Match each animal with its habitat.

3 Compare your matches with a classmate's. Tell why you made the matches you did.

Science Skill

When you classify the cards, you look for ways the pictures go together.

Different Land Habitats

Some land environments have hot weather. Others have cold weather. Some get a lot of rain, and others get very little. In each environment, animals have habitats where they can find what they need.

desert

rain forest

woodland forest

Arctic

Desert Habitats

A **desert** is an environment that gets little rain. Only a few kinds of plants and animals have habitats there. Desert plants and animals do not need much water. Most desert plants store water and use it later. Many desert animals get their water from food.

■ **How are these living things meeting their needs?**

elf owl

saguaro cactus

Gila monster

Rain Forest Habitats

A **rain forest** is an environment where rain falls almost every day. Most rain forests have warm weather all year round. Many plants and animals have habitats there. The plants are used as food and shelter for the animals.

■ **How are these animals meeting their needs?**

emerald tree boa

leaf bats

tree frog

Woodland Forest Habitats

A **woodland forest** is an environment that gets enough rain and warmth for many trees to grow. Animals in forest habitats use the trees and plants for food and shelter.

When the weather turns cold, most of the trees in a woodland forest lose their leaves. Some birds fly to warmer places. Some other animals sleep all winter.

pileated woodpecker

■ **How are these animals meeting their needs?**

raccoons

Arctic Habitats

The **Arctic** is a place with a cold, windy environment. The land is covered with ice and snow for most of the year. The summers are cool and short. A few plants can grow, but the summer is too short for trees to grow.

Only a few animals have habitats in the Arctic because the winter is so cold. The polar bear's thick fur keeps it warm when it goes out to find food.

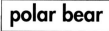

polar bear

Think About It

1. How are land environments alike? How are they different?
2. How do animals meet their needs in their land habitats?

What Are Different Water Habitats?

Investigate

Salt Water and Fresh Water

You will need

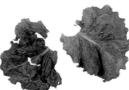

2 cups of
water

2 lettuce
leaves

salt and
spoon

paper and
pencil

1. Mix two spoonfuls of salt into one cup of water.

2. Place a lettuce leaf in each cup of water. Leave the lettuce in the water all night.

3. Predict what will happen to each leaf. Write your predictions. Draw pictures.

4. Check the lettuce the next day. What do you observe? Did you predict correctly?

Science Skill

When you predict, you use what you know to tell what you think will happen.

Different Water Habitats

The Earth has many water environments. A **pond** is a small freshwater environment, and an ocean is a much larger saltwater environment. In each environment, plants and animals have habitats.

pond

ocean

Freshwater Habitats in a Pond

Frogs, birds, otters, and many kinds of insects live along the banks of a pond. Otters and muskrats often build burrows for shelter. Turtles, fish, and water plants live in the pond water.

muskrat

snapping turtle

The surface, or top, of the pond is the habitat of water lilies and other plants. Frogs and turtles use these plants for shelter. Some pond animals, such as insects, use these plants for food.

Some animals use the pond's surface when they look for food. Ducks and water spiders float on the surface. From there they dive to find fish and plants underwater.

■ **Why do you think this spider takes a bubble of air underwater?**

fishing spider

algae

saltwater fish

Saltwater Habitats in the Ocean

An ocean is a large body of salt water. Algae live near the ocean's surface. These plants are food for fish and other ocean animals.

Most ocean animals swim to places where they can find food. Ocean mammals, such as whales and dolphins, must come to the surface to breathe air.

dolphins

bull's-eye lobster

Plants and animals such as lobsters and crabs live on the ocean floor. The parts of the ocean floor that get sunlight have many plants. The animals that live there eat these plants.

Think About It

1. What are some freshwater habitats?
2. What are some saltwater habitats?

A person who studies the ocean is called an oceanographer. Jacques-Yves Cousteau was a famous French oceanographer. He studied the plants and animals that live in the ocean environment.

How Do Plants and Animals Help Each Other?

Investigate

One Way Animals Use Plants

You will need

dish of birdseed

dish of berries

paper and pencil

Do Birds Like Seeds or Berries?		
Like Seeds	Like Berries	Like Both

1 With your teacher, put the food outside where birds can get it.

2 Make a chart like this one. Record what you observe each day.

3 Use your chart to tell what you observed.

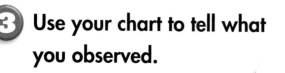
Science Skill
Making a chart helps you keep track of what you observe.

How Animals and Plants Help Each Other

Bees and flowers show one way animals and plants help each other. The bee helps the flower make seeds. The flower makes a sweet liquid called nectar that is food for the bee.

bumble bee

pollen

Plants Help Animals

Many animals eat plant parts. Birds eat seeds and fruits. Pandas and many other mammals eat leaves and stems.

Animals also use plants for shelter. A raccoon may live in a hole in a tree. Many birds use twigs, leaves, and grasses to build nests.

giant panda

■ **How are these animals using plants?**

American bittern

Animals Help Plants

Animals help plants by moving their seeds to new growing places. Birds eat berries that have seeds inside. Later, the seeds fall to the ground in the birds' waste. The seeds may grow into new plants far away from the plant they came from.

Seeds also stick to an animal's fur. When the animal moves, the seeds move with it. When the seeds fall off, they may land in soil and germinate.

cedar waxwing

bison

■ What is this bison doing to help plants?

Food Chains

All living things need food to live and grow. Plants use sunlight to make their food. Some animals eat the plants. Other animals eat the plant eaters. A **food chain** is the order in which animals eat plants and other animals.

The picture shows a food chain in a pond. The food chain begins with the plants on the surface of the pond. A beetle eats the plants, and a fish eats the beetle. Then a blue heron eats the fish.

Think About It

1. How do plants and animals help each other?
2. What is a food chain?

 **Math Link**

How Much Rain?

Rainfall makes a desert and a rain forest what they are. A desert is dry. It may get less than 2 centimeters of rain in a month. A rain forest is wet. It may get more than 16 centimeters of rain in a month.

Think and Do

Measure 2 centimeters from the edge of a sheet of paper, and make a pencil mark. Make another pencil mark at 16 centimeters. How many more centimeters of rain fall in a rain forest than in a desert in a month? Show your answer as a math problem.

Byrd Baylor Observes Deserts

Byrd Baylor writes about the desert. She likes to observe the plants and animals that live there. She writes poems about the desert. One of her books of poems is called *Desert Voices*.

BAYLOR/PARNALL

DESERT VOICES

DESERT VOICES
BY BYRD BAYLOR AND PETER PARNALL

Scribners

Think and Do

Find a poem by Byrd Baylor. Share it with others. Talk about how she wrote about plants and animals. Then write your own poem about a place you enjoy.

Tell What You Know

1. Tell what you know about the picture. Use the words *woodland forest, environment,* and *food chain.*

Vocabulary

Tell which picture goes with the word or words.

2. habitat

3. desert

4. rain forest

5. pond

6. Arctic

a.   b.   c.

d.   e.

Using Science Skills

7. **Communicate** Draw a picture to show a food chain that includes three or more living things. Show your picture to a classmate. Talk about how the food chain works.

8. **Compare** Make a chart like this one to compare land environments. Then make a chart to compare water environments.

Comparing Land Environments			
Environment	Weather	Animals	Plants
desert			
rain forest			
woodland forest			
Arctic			

Changes in Habitats

drought

pollution

litter

reuse

recycle

Did You Know?

If you **recycle** a stack of newspapers that is 4 feet tall, you will keep one tree from being cut down.

How Does Weather Change Habitats?

Investigate

Weather and Seeds

You will need

seeds

2 paper plates

4 wet paper towels

spray bottle

paper and pencil

1. Lay a wet towel on each plate. Put 4 seeds on each towel. Cover with another wet towel.

2. Put the plates in a warm place. Keep the towels on one plate wet.

3. Check the seeds each day. Record what you observe.

4. Draw a conclusion about whether seeds outdoors need rain.

Science Skill
Use your observations and what you know to draw a conclusion.

How Rain Changes the Land

Plants and animals need certain things. Sometimes too little or too much rain changes their habitats. Then plants and animals may not have what they need.

dry wheat fields

Droughts

A pond can dry up when there is no rain for a long time. A long time without rain is called a **drought**. Without enough water, most pond plants die. Many pond animals move to other ponds.

■ How are these ponds different?

■ How is the land in these pictures different?

Floods

When it rains for a long time, rainwater may flood the land. Then the plants and animals get too much water. Plants die and animals move to drier places.

Lightning and Fire

Sometimes lightning strikes a tree in a forest. If the forest is dry, the tree may catch fire. The fire may burn other trees and spread through the forest.

Some animals may die. Other animals may be able to move quickly to safer places.

After a fire burns a forest, some seeds begin to germinate. Birds drop other seeds on the ground. The seeds grow into new plants, and many animals come back. Over time, the forest begins to look the way it did before the fire.

■ **What conclusion can you draw from this picture?**

Think About It

1. How can too little rain or too much rain change an environment?
2. How does a fire change an environment?

How Does Pollution Change Environments?

Investigate

Whether Soil and Sand Can Clean Water

You will need

sand

soil

coffee filter

funnel

container

Colored water

colored water

1 Put the funnel and then the filter in the container, as shown. Add sand and then soil to make a natural filter.

2 Pour the colored water into your sand-and-soil filter. What do you observe?

3 Your filter works the way the soil outside does. Does the sand-and-soil filter clean the colored water?

Science Skill
When you observe, you use your senses to learn what happens.

How Pollution Changes an Environment

Waste that harms land, water, or air is called **pollution**. Pollution also harms the plants and animals that use the land, water, and air.

Land Pollution

When people put trash in a trash can, the trash may be put in a landfill. Trash that is not put in a trash can is called **litter**. Litter hurts plants and animals. It covers up plants so they cannot get light. Animals may eat litter and get sick.

■ How has this garbage dump changed the land?

Air Pollution

Plants and animals need clean air. Air gets dirty, or polluted, when some factories and cars put out smoke and fumes. This air pollution can make plants and animals sick.

■ **What is polluting the air?**

Water Pollution

All living things need clean water. Water pollution changes rivers, lakes, and streams. Waste from factories and other places can harm plants and animals.

Litter thrown into water is another kind of pollution that hurts animals. If animals eat litter, they may get sick. Litter also gets caught around animals' bodies. Then the animals have trouble moving and eating.

■ **How is litter harming this bird?**

Think About It

1. What are some kinds of pollution?
2. How does pollution harm plants and animals?

LESSON 3

How Do People Help the Environment?

Investigate

How Things Can Be Reused

You will need

used things

markers or paint

glue

newspaper

1 Observe the used things. Could you use them to make something new?

2 List the steps you plan to take. Follow your plan.

3 Use your plan to communicate to a classmate how you made something new.

Science Skill

When you list the steps you plan to take, you make it easier to communicate them.

B44

Ways People Help the Environment

People can take care of their environment and keep it clean. They can pick up litter and make less trash. How are these people helping the environment?

Taking Care of the Land

Some people plant trees. These trees may become new homes for animals. The roots of the trees hold the soil so it will not blow away or wash away.

People take care of the land when they put litter in trash cans. In many places, people work together to pick up litter.

■ **How are these people taking care of the land?**

Making less trash is another way people can take care of the land. People decided to **reuse**, or use again, old tires to build this playground.

People also make less trash by recycling. To **recycle** means to use old materials to make new things. Metal cans and plastic bottles may be melted down to make other things.

Taking Care of the Air

People can take care of the air by making less pollution. People sometimes choose to walk or ride bicycles instead of driving their cars everywhere. Many factories have found ways to put less pollution in the air.

■ **What is this person doing to help keep the air clean?**

Taking Care of the Water

People can help keep water clean in rivers, lakes, streams, and oceans. Some people help by picking up litter. Many factory owners are finding ways for their factories to get rid of waste without putting it into the water.

■ **How are these people helping take care of the water?**

Think About It

1. How can people keep the environment clean?

2. What are some ways people can make less pollution?

Math Link

How Much Paper Trash Could You Reuse?

A landfill has many kinds of trash. It may have old bottles, empty cans, and even broken television sets. Paper is what takes up the most space in a landfill.

Think and Do

Keep a large bag at the front of the classroom for one day. Throw all your paper trash in it.

At the end of the day, count the papers you could reuse. Then count the papers you could not reuse. Compare. Are there more papers you could reuse or more papers you could not reuse?

Archaeologists Investigate Trash

Long ago, many people threw their trash into holes in the ground. Today archaeologists dig up the trash in these holes. Archaeologists are scientists who study how people lived long ago.

The trash helps them learn more about the people who threw it away. A broken toy may show that a family had a child. A jar may show what people liked to eat.

Think and Do

Check your classroom trash and make a chart like this one. Write what each piece of trash tells about your class.

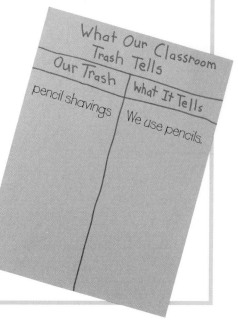

What Our Classroom Trash Tells

Our Trash	What It Tells
pencil shavings	We use pencils.

Tell What You Know

Tell what you know about each picture.

1. **2.** **3.** **4.**

Vocabulary

Match each word with a picture that shows its meaning.

5. pollution

6. recycle

7. litter

8. reuse

a.

b.

c.

d.

Using Science Skills

9. Draw Conclusions These two pictures show the same lake.

before

after

What conclusion can you draw about what happened to the lake?

10. Compare What things do your school and your neighborhood recycle? Make a chart like this one. Compare the things you see being recycled at school and in your neighborhood.

Things I See Recycled		
Objects	School	Neighborhood
Glass Bottles		⦀⦀
Paper	⦀⦀ ‖	‖

Nature Walk

1. Take a nature walk with an adult family member or your class.

2. Observe as many different animals as you can.

3. Take notes. Draw pictures and write about how these animals meet their needs.

4. Share your notes.

Make an Earthworm Habitat

1. Fill a large jar with soil. Sprinkle water on the soil.

2. Place earthworms on the soil.

3. Sprinkle soil and leaves over the earthworms.

4. Observe the habitat for several days. Draw and write to tell how the earthworms use their habitat.

5. Return the earthworms outdoors.

Recycle and Reuse

Make a recycling chart. Show the kinds of things that can be recycled or reused.

See What Is in the Air

1. Spread petroleum jelly on the center of an index card.

2. Place the card outdoors on a windowsill.

3. The next day observe the card with a hand lens.

4. Draw and write about what you see.

5. Put another card in a different place. Do the activity again. Compare what happens.

WRITING
Which kind of environment would you like to visit most? Make a travel poster that tells about it. Include labels.

READING
Squish! A Wetland Walk by Nancy Luenn
Read about plants and animals that live in a wetland. How do wetlands help people? Tell your ideas.

COMPUTER CENTER
Visit **The Learning Site** at www.harcourtschool.com

Exploring Earth's Surface

Earth Science

Exploring Earth's Surface

UNIT PROJECT

What Do You Know?

Make fossil flash cards. Write questions on one side and answers on the other side.

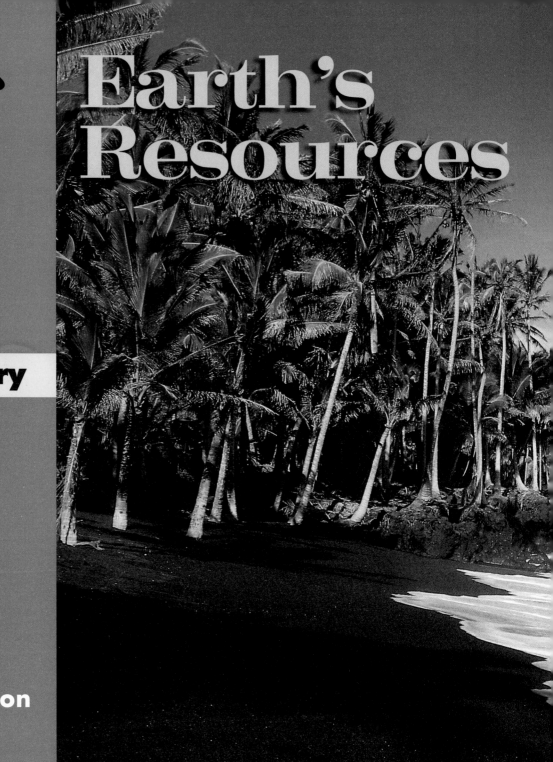

Earth's Resources

Vocabulary

rock

soil

boulder

sand

resource

natural resource

transportation

mineral

Did You Know?

In Hawaii, the black **sand** on some beaches is made up of pieces of **rock** from a nearby volcano.

Did You Know?

Diamond is a **mineral** that is so hard it can scratch glass.

How Do People Use Rocks and Soil?

A Way to Use Soil

You will need

clay

ice cube tray

1 Make some clay bricks. Fill an ice cube tray with clay.

2 Put the tray in a warm, sunny place. Take the bricks out when they are hard.

3 What happened to the bricks? Infer why you put the bricks in the sun.

Science Skill
When you infer information, you can figure out why something happened.

Ways That People Use Rocks and Soil

A **rock** is a hard, nonliving thing that comes from the Earth. The loose top layer of the Earth's surface is **soil**. People use rocks and soil in different ways.

Different Kinds of Rocks

Rocks have different sizes, colors, and shapes. A **boulder** is a large rock. A grain of **sand** is a tiny rock. A rock can be shiny or dull, and it can be smooth or rough. Some rocks are harder than others.

boulder

marble

pumice

granite

basalt

sandstone

obsidian

■ How are these rocks different?

Ways That People Use Rocks

Rocks are a kind of natural resource. A **resource** is anything that people can use. A **natural resource** is something found in nature that people can use to meet their needs.

People use rocks to build things, such as houses and roads. They also use rocks to make sculptures.

People may change the size, shape, and texture, or feel, of rocks. They break big rocks into smaller rocks to make gravel for roads. They make parts of sculptures rough and smooth.

Mount Rushmore

truck dumping gravel

■ How are the rocks in the truck being used?

Kinds of Soil

Different kinds of soil have different things in them. Sandy soil has a lot of sand in it. Topsoil has many bits of dead plants and animals. Clay soil is made up of tiny pieces of rock that stick together easily. The three kinds of soil hold different amounts of water.

■ **Which kind of soil holds the most water? Which kind holds the least?**

topsoil

clay soil

sandy soil

potato field

Ways That People Use Soil

People use soil to grow food and to make bricks. One kind of brick is called adobe. People make a mix of wet clay and straw and shape it into bricks. They use the hard bricks to build things.

adobe building

Think About It

1. How do people use rocks?

2. How do people use soil?

How Do People Use Water?

How You Use Water

How Our Class Uses Water in One Day	
How Our Class Uses Water	How Many Times
drinking	
washing hands	
watering plants	
cleaning	

1 Keep track of the ways your class uses water in one day. Collect the data in a chart.

2 Make a tally mark each time your class uses water. After a day, count the marks.

3 Use your data to answer these questions.
- How many ways did your class use water?
- Which way did your class use water most?

Science Skill
Collecting data is one way to find the answers to your questions.

Ways That People Use Water

Water is a natural resource that people use every day. People drink water, but they also use it for swimming, transportation, and cleaning. How are people using water here?

Uses for Water

People, plants, and animals need water to live and grow. People use water for drinking, cooking, bathing, and watering plants. They also use it for washing clothes, dishes, and cars.

■ **How are these children using water?**

ferry

Hoover Dam

People also use water when they sail boats and ships. Boats and ships are kinds of **transportation**, or ways to move people or things.

Water is also used to make electricity. People build dams on rivers. The flow of the river turns machines that make electricity.

Think About It

1. How do people use water to care for plants and animals?
2. What are some other ways people use water?

What Other Natural Resources Do People Use?

Investigate

Using Plants to Make a Bird Feeder

You will need

milk carton   scissors   plant parts   glue   birdseed

1 With your teacher, cut the top off a milk carton.

CAUTION   Cut carefully.

2 Glue plant parts to the sides and bottom of the carton.

3 Put birdseed in your feeder, and place it outside.

4 Communicate to classmates what you did.

Science Skill

You can show things to **communicate** about them.

Other Natural Resources People Use

Plants and air are two other important natural resources. People use these natural resources to meet their needs. How are these people using plants and air?

How People Use Plants

Plants are a resource that people use to make many products. People use wood from trees to build furniture and houses.

People also use wood to make paper. They make wood chips into a wet, woody mix called pulp. Then they press the pulp flat to make sheets of paper.

- **How have people used plants here?**

pine tree

pine stool

newspapers

People also make cloth from plants. They use the cotton plant to make cloth for clothes, sheets, and many other products.

People also use plants for food. They eat fruits and vegetables. They use other plant parts to make foods such as bread and pasta.

cotton boll

cotton hat

■ How is this boy using plants?

How People Use Minerals

Minerals are another natural resource people use. A **mineral** is one kind of nonliving thing that is found in nature. People find minerals in rocks. Copper, iron, and diamonds are minerals. People use these minerals to make coins, furniture, and jewelry.

■ **What are these minerals used to make?**

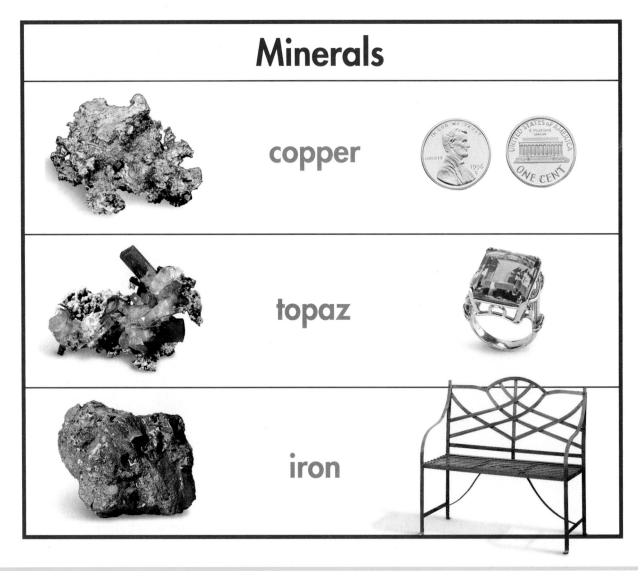

Minerals

copper

topaz

iron

How People Use Air

Air is another important resource. People need clean air to breathe, but they use it in other ways, too. They use air to fill tires, rafts, and toys. They also use air when they fly in airplanes.

■ **How is this girl using air?**

Think About It

1. What are some ways people use plants?

2. What are some other resources people use?

Math Link

How Much Water?

Most people use about 100 gallons of water each day. They use the water for drinking, keeping clean, and cooking. They also use it for washing clothes, dishes, and pets.

Think and Do

It takes about 2 gallons of water to wash your hands and face. If 4 people in a family wash their hands and faces, how much water will they use? Write an addition problem to show the answer.

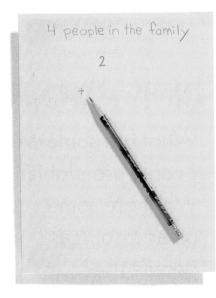

4 people in the family

2

+

An Artist Uses Natural Resources

Maya Lin is an architect and artist who works with stone and other natural materials. She has designed sculptures made of granite and has even used water in her work. Lin designed an earth sculpture called "The Wave Field." It is made of soil covered with grass.

Think and Do

Design your own sculpture. First draw a picture of what your sculpture will look like. Use rocks, clay, soil, leaves and other natural materials to make your sculpture.

Tell What You Know

1. How does the picture show ways people use natural resources?

Vocabulary

Tell which picture goes with each word.

2. minerals

3. boulder

4. soil

5. sand

a.

b.

c.

d.

Using Science Skills

6. **Make Models/Communicate**

Make a model boat to show one way people use water. Decide what you will use to make your model. You could use clay, paper, or an empty milk carton.

Write one sentence that tells how your model boat uses water. Write another sentence that tells what resources you used to make it.

7. **Collect Data/Communicate**

Make a chart to show ways people use three resources. Draw or cut out pictures that show some ways that each resource is used. Glue your pictures in the chart. Then share your chart.

How People Use Resources		
Rocks	Plants	Water

Earth Long Ago

Vocabulary

fossil
paleontologist
reconstruct
dinosaur
extinct
Triceratops

Did You Know?

Plant-eating **dinosaurs** were the largest land animals that ever lived on Earth.

Did You Know?

The moa was a bird 10 feet tall that became **extinct** about 300 years ago.

What Is a Fossil?

Investigate

How Some Fossils Get Their Shapes

You will need

clay

small objects

1 Break the clay into four pieces. Press each piece flat.

2 Press a different object into each piece to make a print. Remove the object.

3 Have classmates infer which object made each print.

Science Skill
You can use clues to infer information.

Fossils

Plants and animals lived on the Earth before people did. People know this because they have found fossils. A **fossil** is what is left of a plant or an animal that lived long ago.

fossil

How Fossils Are Made

Some plants and animals that died millions of years ago were eaten. Many rotted away. Other plants and animals became fossils.

These pictures show one way fossils are made. A fish in the ocean dies. Its body sinks to the ocean floor. Soon the fish is covered up with mud.

fish fossil

■ **What is happening to the fish's body?**

How a Fossil Is Made

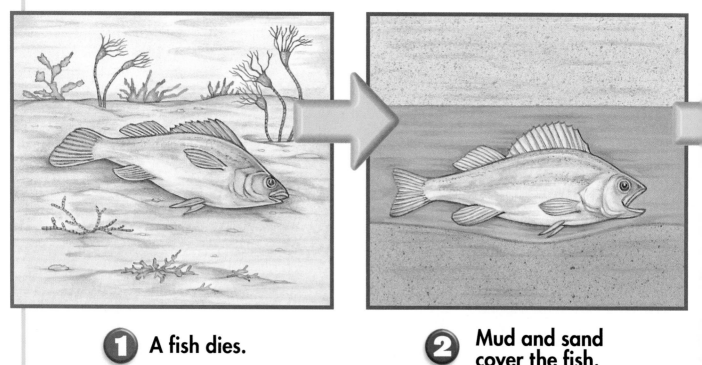

1 A fish dies.

2 Mud and sand cover the fish.

A **paleontologist** is a scientist who finds and studies fossils. By studying fossils, a paleontologist learns about plants and animals that lived long ago.

More mud and sand cover the fish's body as it rots away. They press on the mud for a long time until this mud turns to rock. A print of the fish is left in the rock. Prints like this are one kind of fossil.

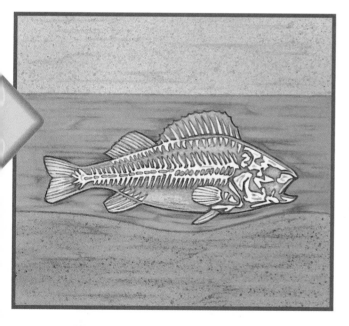

 3 The mud and sand turn to rock.

■ **What is this paleontologist doing?**

Where Fossils Are Found

Scientists find many kinds of fossils in rocks. Some are animal teeth, shells, and bones that have turned to stone. Others are plant and animal prints.

footprint fossil

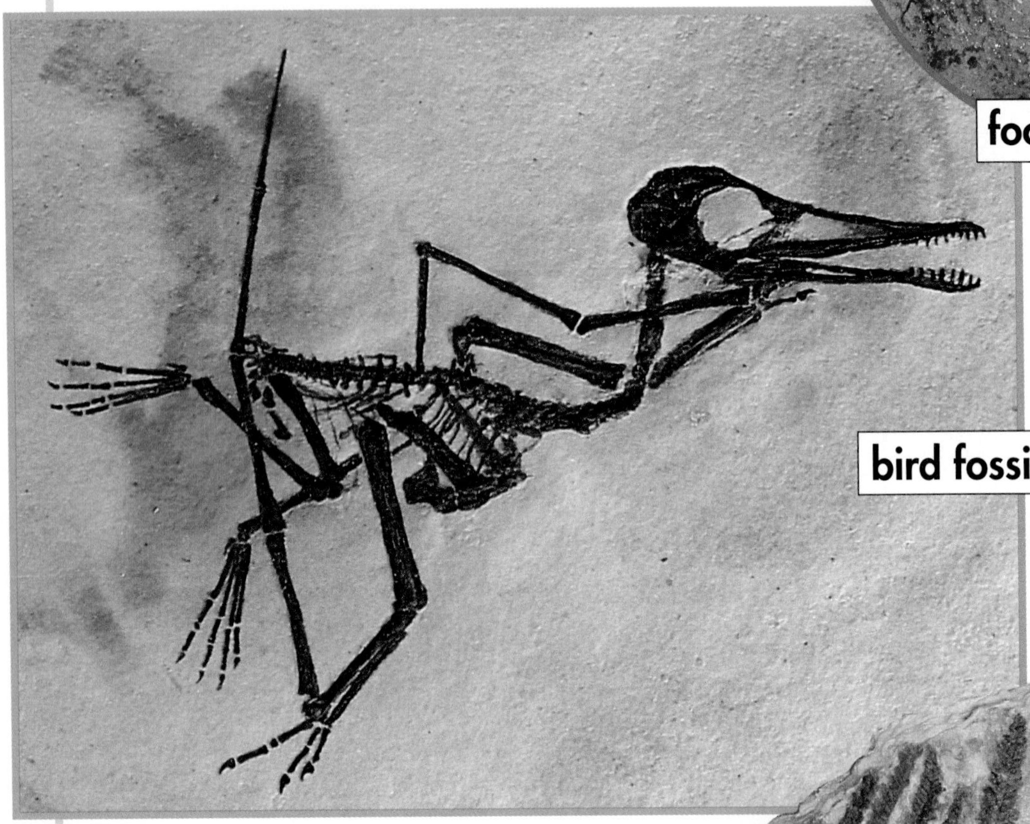

bird fossil

■ What kind of fossil is this?

Scientists also find fossils in other things, such as tar and amber. Amber is the hard sap of pine trees that grew long ago.

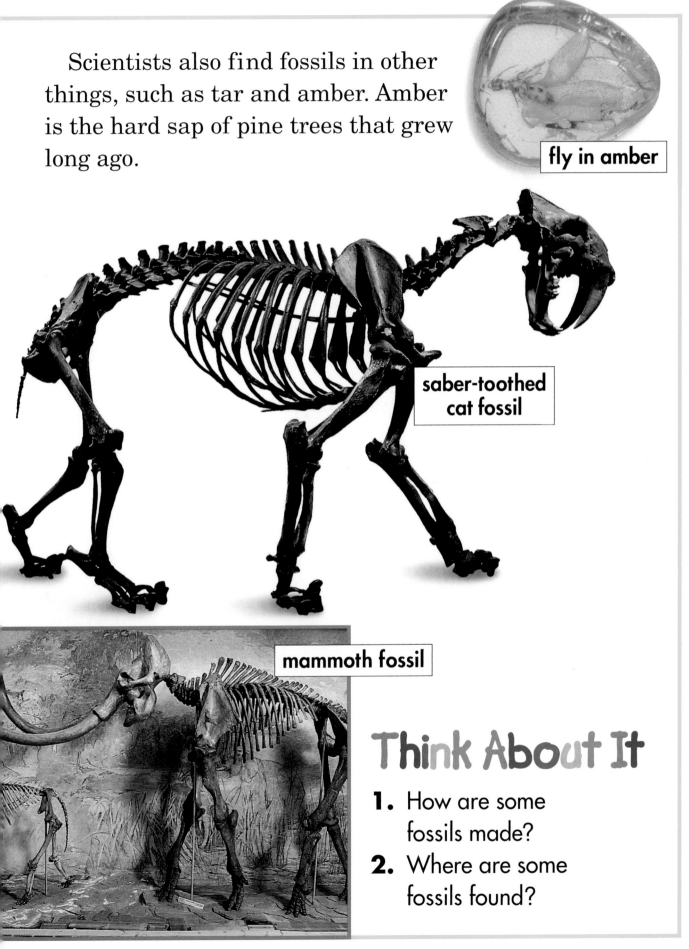

fly in amber

saber-toothed cat fossil

mammoth fossil

Think About It

1. How are some fossils made?
2. Where are some fossils found?

How Do Scientists Get Fossils?

How Scientists Find Fossils

You will need

play dough

small objects

tools

1 Hide an object in some play dough. Let the dough get hard. Trade with a classmate.

2 Use tools to find the object. Do not harm the object.

3 Communicate what you did.

Science Skill
One way to communicate is to talk with your partner about what you did.

How Scientists Get Fossils

Scientists find some fossils inside rocks. To get the fossils out, they must chip the rock away. They work slowly and carefully so that they do not break the fossils.

How Scientists Put Fossils Together

When scientists chip a fossil from a rock, it may be in pieces. They take the fossil pieces to a museum, where they first clean them.

Then the scientists try to put the fossil together. They look at the pieces and use what they know about animals. They want to **reconstruct**, or rebuild, as much of the skeleton as possible.

Putting Fossils Together

1 The fossil is taken out of the rock.

2 The pieces are cleaned.

What Scientists Learn from Fossils

Afrovenator fossil

Fossils help scientists learn about plants and animals that lived long ago. Scientists also learn from fossils how plants and animals have changed. They compare the fossils with plants and animals that live today.

3 The fossil pieces are put together.

■ Observe the fossil above. How do you think the living animal looked?

Think About It

1. How do scientists get fossils?
2. What do scientists learn from fossils?

What Have Scientists Learned About Dinosaurs?

Dinosaur Skeletons

You will need

scissors

books about
dinosaurs

chenille sticks

1 Choose a dinosaur to make a model skeleton.

2 Twist two chenille sticks together. Shape them to make the backbone and the head.

3 Twist sticks around the backbone for legs. Cut and twist on more sticks for ribs.

✂ Cut carefully.
CAUTION

Science Skill
Sharing your model can help you explain your ideas.

What Scientists Know About Dinosaurs

A **dinosaur** is an animal that lived millions of years ago. Today dinosaurs are **extinct**, or no longer living. Paleontologists know about dinosaurs from their fossils.

dinosaur fossil

Kinds of Dinosaurs

Many kinds of dinosaurs used to live on the Earth. Some were as small as a chicken. Others were taller than a three-story building.

The word *dinosaur* means "terrible lizard." Paleontologists give each dinosaur a name that describes it. One kind of dinosaur is named **Triceratops**, which means "three-horned face."

Another dinosaur is named Tyrannosaurus rex. Its name means "tyrant lizard king." A tyrant is a mean ruler. Tyrannosaurus rex was one of the fiercest dinosaurs of all.

How Tall Were Dinosaurs?

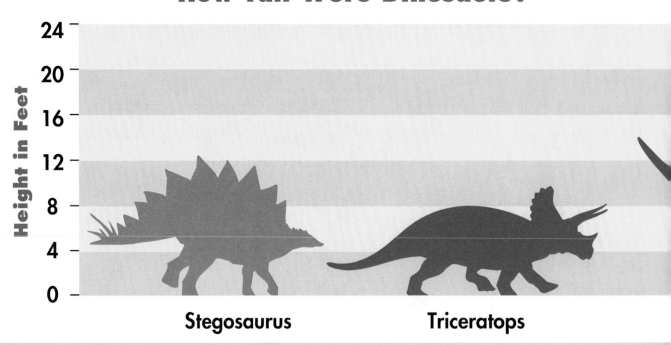

Stegosaurus   Triceratops

■ How tall was Tyrannosaurus rex?

Tyrannosaurus rex   Diplodocus   child, age 7

What Scientists Learn About Dinosaurs

One way paleontologists learn about dinosaurs is by comparing them to animals that live today. Triceratops had flat teeth like those of today's plant-eating animals. Tyrannosaurus rex had long, pointed teeth like those of today's meat eaters.

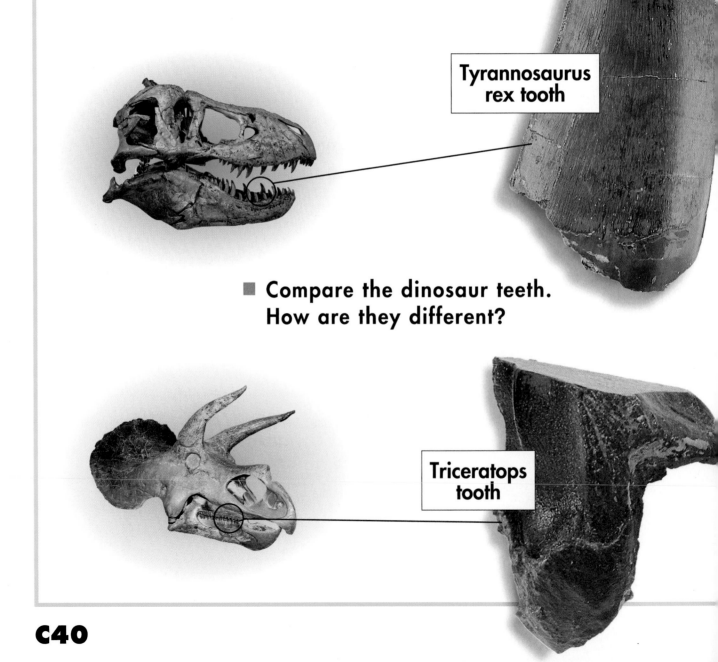

Tyrannosaurus rex tooth

■ Compare the dinosaur teeth. How are they different?

Triceratops tooth

Scientists have found fossil prints of dinosaur skin. These fossils show that some dinosaurs had scaly skin. Others had smoother skin.

dinosaur skin

Scientists know that some dinosaurs laid eggs. Fossil dinosaur nests have been found with fossils of eggs in them. Scientists have also found fossils of young dinosaurs around some nests.

■ **What is in this dinosaur nest?**

Think About It

1. How do scientists learn about dinosaurs?
2. What have scientists found out about dinosaurs?

Math Link

Compare Dinosaur Sizes

Scientists know from fossils that dinosaurs were many sizes. Compsognathus was about 2 feet long. Scelidosaurus was about 12 feet long. Stegosaurus was larger. It was about 20 feet long.

Compsognathus

Scelidosaurus

Stegosaurus

Think and Do

Make a bar graph to compare the lengths of these dinosaurs. Then use your graph to talk about which dinosaur was the longest and which was the shortest.

Dinosaur Lengths										
Compsognathus										
Scelidosaurus										
Stegosaurus										

0 2 4 6 8 10 12 14 16 18 20

No More Brontosaurus

Paleontologists found fossils of a kind of dinosaur they named Apatosaurus. Then they found bone fossils that looked the same but were bigger. They thought they had found a different kind of dinosaur and called it Brontosaurus.

Later, scientists figured out that both sets of fossils were from Apatosaurus bones. The name Brontosaurus is not used anymore.

Think and Do

Find out what it might be like to fit fossils together. Draw two pictures of the same kind of animal, but make one larger. Cut out each body part. Mix up the body parts of both animals. Trade with a classmate. Try to put each of your classmate's two pictures together.

Tell What You Know

1. Tell what you know about each picture.

Vocabulary

Use these words to tell about the picture.

2. fossil

3. dinosaur

4. extinct

5. Triceratops

6. paleontologist

Using Science Skills

7. Make a Model This is a trilobite fossil. A trilobite was an animal that lived in the ocean millions of years ago. It was about 8 to 10 centimeters, or 3 to 4 inches, long.

Use clay and a pencil tip to make a model of a trilobite fossil. Use your model to tell a classmate about trilobites.

8. Infer The table shows the teeth of two dinosaurs. Copy the table. Write what each dinosaur ate and how you know.

Dinosaur Teeth and What Dinosaurs Ate			
Dinosaur	Shape of Tooth	What It Ate	How I Know
Tyrannosaurus			
Triceratops			

Make Watercolor Pictures

1. Paint a picture with watercolor paint. Let the painting dry.

2. Observe the paper. What has happened to the water in the paint? How can you tell?

3. Write about what you observe.

Soil Nutrients Study

1. With an adult, collect once-living things such as a berry, a stick, and a leaf.

2. Bury each object outside in its own hole about 4 inches deep.

3. Mark each spot. Check the objects once a week for four weeks.

4. Record what you observe.

5. Draw a conclusion.

Water in Soil

1. Place some soil on a paper towel.

2. Let it stand for half an hour.

3. Shake off the soil. What is left on the towel?

4. Communicate your findings to classmates.

Make a Rock Collection

1. Collect some small rocks.

2. Observe the rocks and decide how you want to classify them.

3. Glue the rocks in groups on pieces of cardboard. Label each group.

4. Share your rock collection.

light colored rocks

dark colored rocks

WRITING

Track Facts Choose a dinosaur to learn more about. Write facts. Draw its picture on a dinosaur footprint. Add your writing to a class "dinosaur trail."

READING

Fossils Tell of Long Ago **by Aliki**

What kinds of fossils have people found on mountains? Share what you learn.

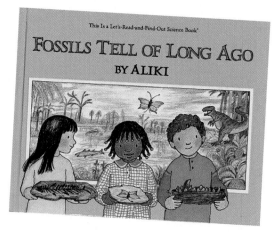

COMPUTER CENTER

Visit *The Learning Site* at www.harcourtschool.com

Space and Weather

Space and Weather

UNIT PROJECT

Weather Station

Keep track of the weather. Set up a classroom weather station.

CHAPTER 1

The Sun, the Moon, and Stars

Vocabulary

sun
energy
solar energy
rotation
orbit
season
moon
moonlight
crater
constellation

Did You Know?
The **sun** is so large that more than a million Earths could fit inside it.

Did You Know?

The **moon** has no air or water, and the sky is always black.

What Causes Day and Night?

Where the Sun Is

You will need

paper and pencil

Where the Sun Is			
	Day 1	Day 2	Day 3
10:00 a.m.			
2:00 p.m.			

 1 Observe where the sun is in the morning. Record.

CAUTION Never look directly at the sun.

2 Observe the sun from the same place in the afternoon. Record where it is now.

3 Observe the sun at the same times for 2 more days. Record.

4 What pattern do you see?

Science Skill

A pattern of something happening over and over at the same place and time is a time/space relationship.

Day and Night

Each day, the sun seems to move across the sky. The sun does not really cross our sky. It is Earth that is moving. Because Earth moves, we have day and night.

sunrise

noon

sunset

The Sun

The **sun** is the star closest to Earth. The sun is much larger than Earth. It looks small only because it is far away.

The sun is made of hot gases. The gases are so hot they give off light and heat. Light and heat are kinds of **energy** because they can cause change and do work.

sun

Most living things on Earth use **solar energy**, or light and heat from the sun. Plants use the sun's light to make food. Animals and people use its light to see in the daytime. The sun's heat warms water, land, air, and all living things on Earth.

■ **What does the sun look like here?**

Earth's Rotation

Earth is shaped something like a sphere, or a ball. It spins round and round in space. The spinning of Earth is called its **rotation**. It takes about 24 hours for Earth to rotate, or spin, all the way around one time. One full rotation of Earth is one full day.

United States

day

Austin, Texas
day

■ **Which part of Earth is having day here?**

The sun shines all the time, but not always on your part of Earth. Earth's rotation causes each part of Earth to have light and dark each day.

When one side of Earth faces the sun, that side is lighted, and it is daytime. The other side of Earth is dark, and it is nighttime.

United States

night

Austin, Texas
night

Think About It

1. What is the sun?

2. Why does Earth have day and night?

What Causes the Seasons?

Investigate

How Sunlight Shines on Earth

You will need

ball with
pencil

lamp

1 Tilt the ball so the top
of the pencil points
toward the light.

2 Does the light shine
more brightly on the
top or the bottom of
the ball? Record.

3 Move the ball to the other side of the light.
Keep the tilt of the pencil the same.

4 Observe where the light is
brightest now. Record and discuss.

Science Skill
To observe light here,
you need only your
sense of sight.

What Causes the Seasons

Earth rotates on an imaginary line called an axis. Earth tilts on this axis. At the same time, Earth moves around the sun. For these reasons, Earth has different seasons.

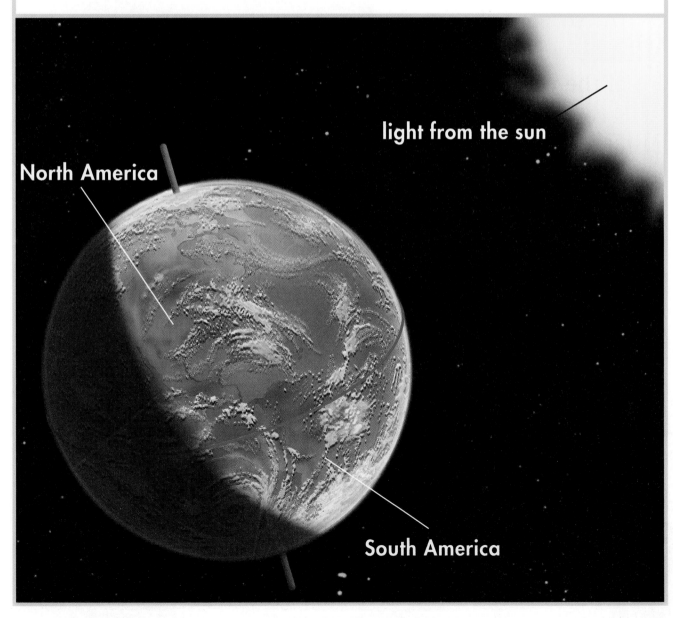

light from the sun

North America

South America

Earth Orbits the Sun

Earth moves in an **orbit**, or a path, around the sun. It takes Earth one year to orbit the sun. As Earth orbits the sun, the seasons change. A **season** is a time of the year that has a certain kind of weather.

Earth

fall

sun

winter

■ Observe where Earth is in summer. Where has it moved to in winter?

summer

spring

Why the Seasons Change

Earth is always tilted in the same direction. When Earth is on one side of the sun, part of Earth faces the sun directly and gets more direct sunlight. This part of Earth has summer.

- Is the tilt of Earth the same or different in spring and summer?

spring

summer

When Earth moves to the other side of the sun, Earth still tilts in the same direction. Now the tilt causes this same part of Earth to face the sun on a slant. Sunlight does not hit Earth as directly. This part of Earth has winter.

Think About It

1. How does Earth move around the sun?
2. Why do the seasons change?

fall

winter

How Does the Moon Move and Change?

Light from the Moon

You will need

foam ball   foil   pencil   flashlight

1 With a partner, cover the ball with foil. Push the pencil into it to make a handle.

2 Observe how the ball looks in the dark. Draw it.

3 Hold the ball by the handle. Have your partner shine the flashlight on the ball. Draw and compare.

Science Skill

When you compare, you tell how two things are alike and different.

Moonlight

The **moon** is the largest object you can see in the night sky. It seems to shine, but the moon does not really give off its own light. The light from the moon, or **moonlight**, comes from the sun.

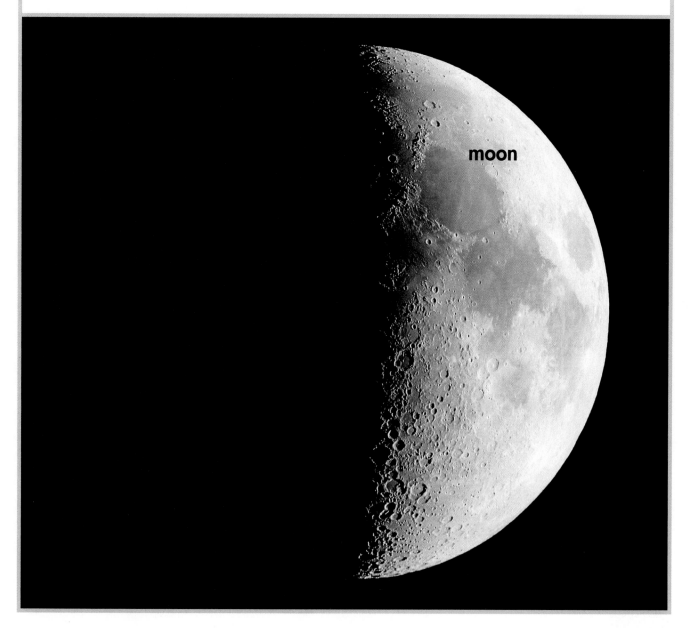

moon

The Moon

The moon is a huge ball of rock that orbits Earth. It takes about 29 days for the moon to orbit Earth.

When we look at the moon, it seems to have spots. Some spots are holes called craters. A **crater** is made when a large rock moving through space hits the moon.

■ **Which part of the moon is lighted by the sun?**

Earth

moon

sun

crater

Astronauts explore space and have gone to the moon. They have seen the craters and the gray dust that covers the moon. They have brought moon rocks back to Earth. Astronaut David Scott commanded the *Apollo 15* mission to the moon.

■ **What do you think this astronaut saw?**

The Moon Seems to Change Shape

The moon's orbit makes the moon seem to change shape. At the start of the moon's orbit, the moon is between the sun and Earth. The sun shines directly on the part of the moon that faces it. We cannot see this new moon from Earth.

In one week, the moon is one-fourth, or one-quarter, of the way through its orbit. From Earth the moon looks like a half-circle.

In two weeks, the moon is halfway around its orbit. Now Earth is between the sun and the moon. From Earth the moon looks like a full circle.

In three weeks, the moon is three-fourths of the way around again. In four weeks, the moon is back where it started.

new moon

■ **Why can't we see the new moon?**

full
moon

quarter
moon

Think About It

1. What makes the moon seem to shine?
2. Why does the moon seem to change shape?

What Can We See in the Night Sky?

Investigate

Star Pictures

You will need

"star" cups

flashlight

black paper

tape

1 Tape the paper to a wall, and choose a star cup.

2 Point the bottom of the cup toward the paper.

3 Shine the flashlight through the cup. What do you see? Record.

4 Repeat with the other cups. Communicate to classmates what you observe.

Science Skill

When you communicate, you tell others what you think through writing, drawing, or speaking.

The Night Sky

On a clear night, you can see many stars.
They look like small points of light in the night
sky. Stars are really much bigger than Earth.
They look small because they are far away.

Stars and Planets

Stars are big balls of hot gases. The hot gases give off light. This light is what we see from Earth. Stars may appear to twinkle.

Some stars seem brighter than others. They may look brighter because they are bigger or hotter. They may also look brighter because they are closer to Earth.

■ **What else might you see in the night sky?**

comet

Milky Way

planet Mars

You may also see planets in the night sky. Planets may look larger and brighter than stars, and they do not twinkle. They do not give off their own light, as stars do.

Some people use telescopes to look at the night sky. A telescope makes things look closer and larger.

■ **How might stars look through a telescope?**

Constellations

Long ago, people saw groups of stars that seemed to form pictures. They named the different star pictures. A group of stars that form a star picture is called a **constellation**.

Little Dipper

Big Dipper

The entire sky has about 88 constellations. One constellation is called the Big Dipper. It is a group of seven stars. Together, they form the shape of a dipper, a kind of big spoon.

Orion the Hunter

■ **What do the constellations on the left look like?**

Think About It

1. What are some things you can see in the night sky?
2. What is a constellation?

Math Link

Use a Calendar

Most places on Earth have four seasons. Each season begins on about the same day every year. Most calendars show the date when each season begins.

Think and Do

Make a chart like this one. Look at a calendar to find when each season begins. Write the date. Then look at the diagram on pages D12 and D13. Draw a picture in your chart to show where Earth is in relation to the sun in each season.

Where Earth Is in Different Seasons		
Season	When It Begins	Where Earth Is
spring		☼
summer		☼
fall		☼
winter		☼

Finding the North Star

For hundreds of years, sailors used stars to find their way. The most important star for them was the North Star. Sailors knew that when they looked at the North Star, they were facing north.

Think and Do

Find the North Star the same way sailors did. First, look at the Big Dipper in the picture.

Big Dipper

Little Dipper

Next, find the two stars on the front of its cup. They line up with the Little Dipper. Last, find the bright star at the end of the handle of the Little Dipper. That is the North Star.

Tell What You Know

1. Use the picture to tell about the moon and why it seems to change shape. Use the words *sun, moonlight, moon,* and *crater.*

Vocabulary

Use the words to tell about each picture.

2.

sun
solar energy

3.

rotation

4.

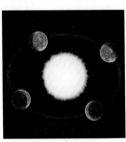

orbit
season

5.

constellation

Using Science Skills

6. Compare Think about summer and winter where you live. Is it warmer in summer or in winter? Are there more hours of daylight in the summer or in winter? How do you know?

Write three sentences that compare summer and winter. You may draw pictures, too.

7. Use Time/Space Relationship The moon orbits Earth in about 29 days. As the moon moves, it seems to change shape. Choose three pictures of the moon from pages D20 and D21. For each one, draw a picture to show where the sun, the moon, and Earth are when the moon looks that way.

CHAPTER 2

Earth's Weather

Vocabulary

weather
water cycle
evaporate
water vapor
thermometer
temperature
stratus
cirrus
cumulus

Did You Know?

The highest **temperature** recorded in the United States was 134°F (about 57°C) in Death Valley, California, on July 10, 1913.

Did You Know?

The windiest and coldest **weather** on Earth is in Antarctica.

How Does Weather Change?

Investigate

Changes in the Weather

You will need

paper

markers

Weather	
Monday	
Tuesday	
Wednesday	
Thursday	
Friday	

1 Make a weather chart like the one above.

2 Observe the weather each day. Record what you observe.

3 What kinds of weather changes did you observe? Share your information.

Science Skill

When you observe weather, you can use sight, hearing, smell, and touch.

Learn About

Changes in Weather

What the air is like outside is **weather**. The air may be warm or cool. It may also be rainy, sunny, windy, or cloudy. Weather can change quickly.

Spring

In many places, the weather changes from season to season. In spring the air gets warmer. In some places, spring is rainy, too. The warmer, wetter weather helps plants grow new leaves and flowers.

■ **What is the spring weather like in these pictures?**

Summer

Summer is the warmest time of the year. Summer days are often hot and sunny. In some places, thunderstorms make the weather change quickly.

■ **How might the weather change here? How do you know?**

Fall

In fall the air gets cooler. Some fall days are cloudy, but others are sunny and clear. In fall the leaves of some trees change color and then drop off. Some plants die.

■ **How is the weather different on these fall days?**

Winter

Winter is the coldest time of the year. In many places, it gets cold enough for snow. In these places, many trees and bushes have bare branches.

In other places, it cools down just a little in winter. These places may rarely have snow. Many trees there stay green, and flowers keep growing.

Think About It

1. How does the weather change from day to day?
2. How does the weather change from season to season?

What Is the Water Cycle?

Water in the Air

You will need

2 zip-top bags

colored water

tape

1 Fill each bag halfway with water. Zip the bags closed.

2 Tape one bag to a window in the sun. Tape the other bag to a window in the shade.

3 After 30 minutes, observe both bags. Which bag shows more change?

4 Infer what caused the change.

Science Skill

When you infer, you think about what you observed and figure out what happened.

The Water Cycle

Water moves from the air to the land and back to the air. The way water keeps doing this over and over is called the **water cycle**.

How the Water Cycle Works

 The drops of water come together and form clouds.

 The water vapor condenses, or changes into tiny drops of water.

2 **This gas, or water vapor, meets cool air.**

 The sun's heat makes water evaporate, or change into a gas.

ocean

5 The water drops become heavy and fall as rain or snow.

mountain

6 The rain and melted snow flow into streams, lakes, and oceans.

stream

Think About It

1. What is the water cycle?

2. How does water get into the air?

How Do We Measure Weather Conditions?

Investigate

Temperature Outside

You will need

thermometer

paper and pencil

Temperature	
Monday	
Tuesday	
Wednesday	
Thursday	
Friday	

 1 Make a chart like this one.

2 At the same time each day, read the thermometer. Record the temperature.

3 Use your data to answer these questions. Did the temperature go up? down? What pattern do you see?

Science Skill

You can use data to look for a pattern of temperature.

Measuring Weather Conditions

Weather conditions can be measured with tools. Some tools tell how hot the air is. Others tell how fast the wind is blowing or how much rain has fallen.

How Scientists Measure Weather Conditions

Scientists called meteorologists use tools to measure weather conditions. A **thermometer** measures temperature. **Temperature** is a measure of how hot or cold the air is. Scientists use rain gauges to measure how much rain or snow has fallen.

An anemometer measures how fast the wind is blowing. A wind vane shows which way the wind is blowing. It points to the direction the wind is coming from.

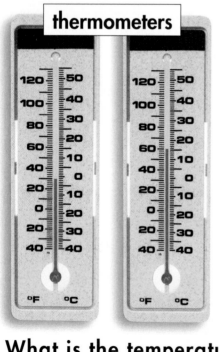

thermometers

wind vane

■ **What is the temperature on each thermometer?**

rain gauge

weather station

Measuring weather conditions helps people know how to dress when they go outside. It also helps scientists see patterns and predict the weather. They can tell people to get ready if a big storm is on the way.

Clouds and the Weather

Looking at clouds is another way people predict the weather. Clouds give clues about how the weather may change.

Stratus, cirrus, and cumulus are three kinds of clouds. The low, gray clouds that stretch across the sky are **stratus** clouds. They usually bring rain or snow. The thin, feathery clouds high in the sky are **cirrus** clouds. We may see cirrus clouds when the weather is sunny.

stratus clouds

■ What kind of weather will the stratus clouds bring?

cumulus clouds

cirrus clouds

The clouds that look like puffy, white cotton are **cumulus** clouds. We see them in fair weather. When cumulus clouds pile up and turn dark, they can bring a thunderstorm.

Think About It

1. How can we measure weather conditions?
2. How can clouds help us predict the weather?

Math Link

Measure Rain

This rain gauge measures how much rain falls. It is used by meteorologists, or weather scientists, at the National Weather Service. The gauge has a bottle that collects rain. It also has a ruler that measures how many inches of rain fall.

A meteorologist checks the rain gauge every day and puts the data into a computer. Then newspapers and television stations use this information for their weather reports.

Think and Do

Measure how much rain falls. Make a rain gauge like this one. Put your rain gauge outside before it rains. When the rain stops, read it. The ruler will show how much rain fell. Record and report your data.

A Poem About Weather

Poets use words to make pictures in the minds of their readers. These word pictures are poems. A poet named Robert Louis Stevenson wrote this poem.

Rain

The rain is raining all around,
It falls on field and tree,
It rains on the umbrellas here,
And on the ships at sea.

Think and Do

Write a poem about the kind of weather you like best. Use the picture in your mind to help you choose words. Read your poem to a classmate. Can your classmate see the picture your poem makes?

REVIEW

Tell What You Know

1. What is the weather like in this season?

2. How can you use this tool to measure weather conditions?

3. If you see these clouds, what kind of weather may be coming?

Vocabulary

Use the words to complete the sentences.

cirrus   **water cycle**   **thermometer**   **stratus**
temperature   **cumulus**   **evaporates**

4. A _____ measures the _____, or how warm the air is.

5. Three kinds of clouds are _____, _____, and _____.

6. The way water moves from the land to the air and back again is called the _____.

7. When water _____, it changes into water vapor.

Using Science Skills

8. Observe/Predict Look out a window at the clouds. What kind of clouds are they? What kind of weather do you think is coming? Write what you predict on a sheet of paper. The next day, see if you were correct.

Use clouds to predict the weather for five days in a row. How many times were you correct?

9. Observe/Collect Data Look outside each day for five days. Observe how hard the wind is blowing. Then use the pictures to find out what kind of wind it is. Record your data in a chart.

| no wind | breeze | wind | strong wind |

Trace Your Shadow

1. On a sunny morning, ask a partner to use chalk to trace your shadow on a sidewalk.

2. Write the time of day on your shadow, and predict how your shadow will look later in the day.

3. In the afternoon, trace a new shadow. Compare.

Which Paper Towel Dries First?

1. With a family member or a classmate, wet three paper towels.

2. Put each towel in a different place.

3. Predict which towel will dry first.

4. Check the towels every 15 minutes. Which one dries first? last? Why?

Observe the Night Sky

1. With an adult, go outside on a clear night.

2. Find the moon. What shape is it?

3. Draw pictures of what you observe.

4. Do the activity again in one week.

5. Communicate how your pictures are different and why.

Make Sun Prints

1. Cut two shapes from construction paper.

2. Place the shapes on black paper.

3. With an adult, go outside. Leave one sheet of black paper in the shade and the other one in the sun.

4. After several hours, remove the cutouts from the black paper. Observe. Why do you think this happens?

WRITING

Flash Cards Write questions on cards to share with classmates. Write the question on one side and the answer on the other.

READING

Sun Up, Sun Down by Gail Gibbons
How does the sun help change the weather? Share "sunny facts" with classmates.

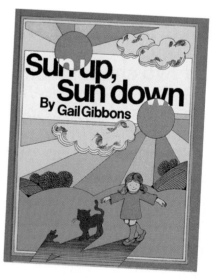

COMPUTER CENTER
Visit *The Learning Site* at
www.harcourtschool.com

Exploring Matter

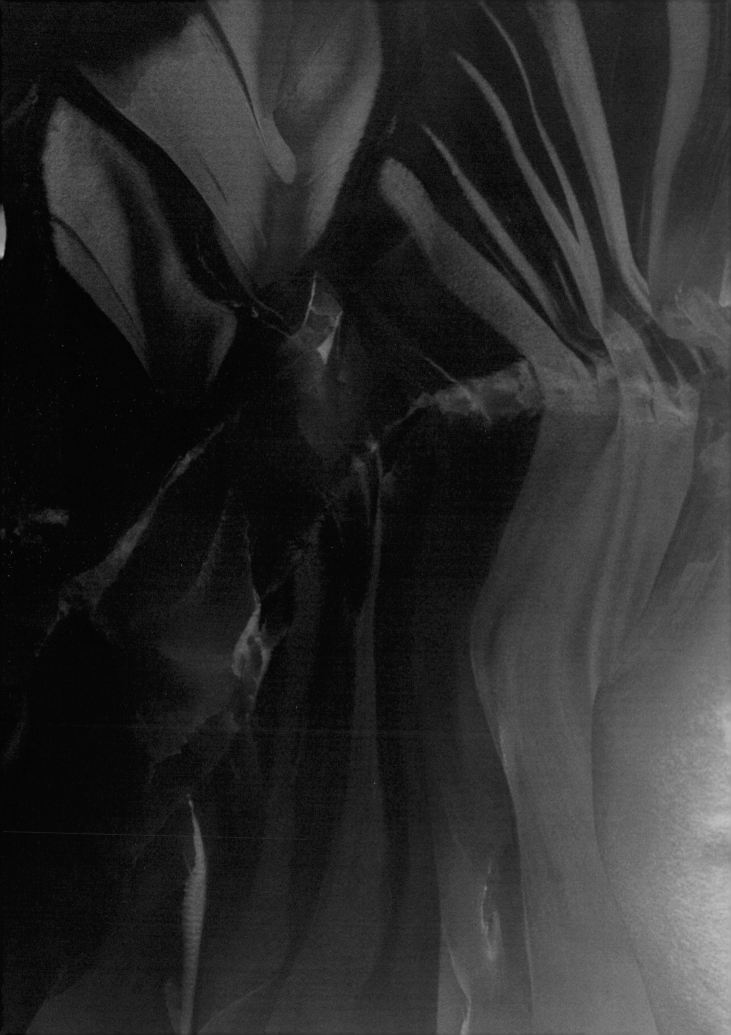

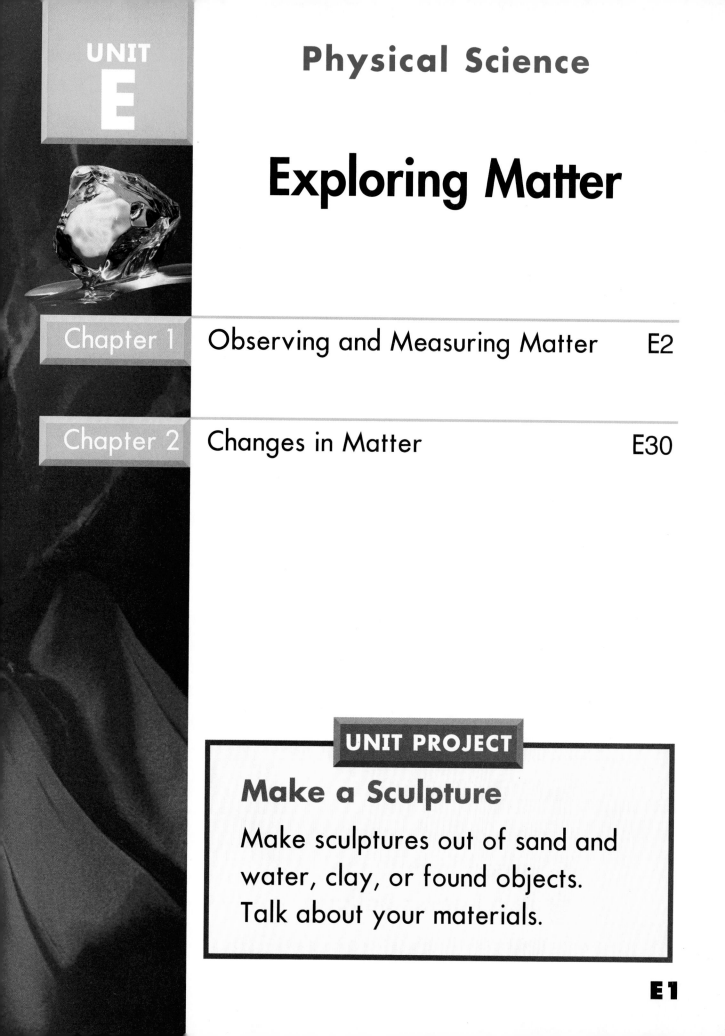

UNIT
E

Physical Science

Exploring Matter

UNIT PROJECT

Make a Sculpture

Make sculptures out of sand and
water, clay, or found objects.
Talk about your materials.

CHAPTER 1

Observing and Measuring Matter

E2

Vocabulary

matter
property
mass
solid
centimeter
liquid
milliliter
gas

Did You Know?

A **gas** called propane is burned to heat the air in a hot-air balloon.

Did You Know?

A **solid** that weighs 100 pounds on Earth would weigh only 17 pounds on the moon.

What Is Matter?

Matter

You will need

3 balls or markers   paper and pencil

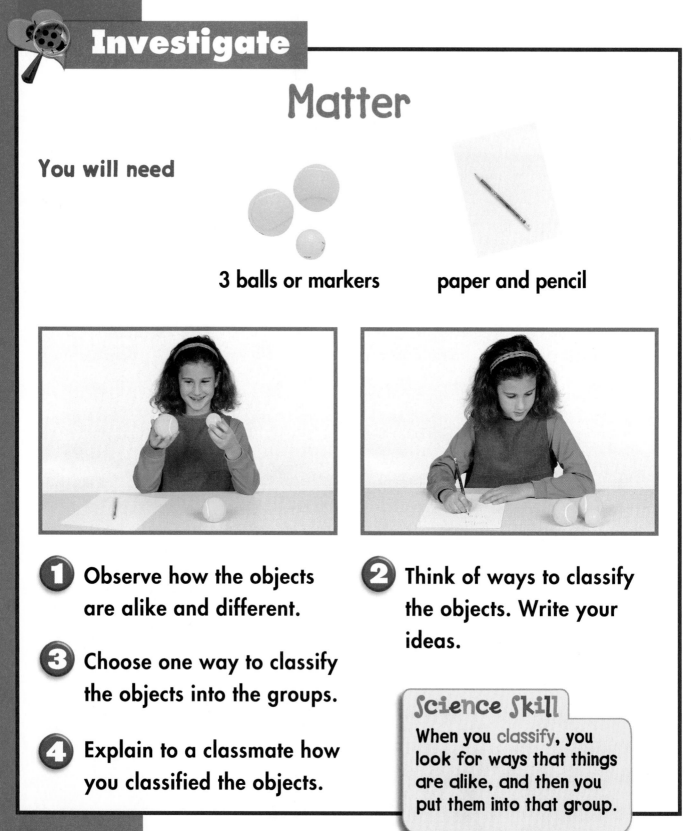

1 Observe how the objects are alike and different.

2 Think of ways to classify the objects. Write your ideas.

3 Choose one way to classify the objects into the groups.

4 Explain to a classmate how you classified the objects.

Science Skill

When you classify, you look for ways that things are alike, and then you put them into that group.

Matter

Matter is what all things are made of. Trees, milk, and air are all made of matter. Even you are made of matter! What different kinds of matter do you see here?

Forms of Matter

Matter has three forms. It can be a solid, a liquid, or a gas. The party hats, the bowl, and the chair are solids. The juice in the bowl is a liquid. The air in the balloons is a gas.

solids

■ How are the objects on these two pages alike and different?

liquid

Properties of Matter

Matter has certain properties. A **property** is a quality of something. Color, size, and shape are properties of matter.

Two other properties of matter are that it takes up space and that it has mass. An object's **mass** is the amount of matter it has.

gas

Think About It

1. What is matter, and what are its forms?

2. What are some properties of matter?

What Can We Find Out About Solids?

 **Investigate**

Solids

You will need

4 objects

balance

paper and pencil

1 Use the balance to find the mass of each object.

2 Put the objects in order from the one with the least mass to the one with the most mass.

3 Make a chart that shows the objects in order from the one with the least mass to the one with the most mass.

Science Skill
When you put objects in order, you can arrange them from least to most.

Solids

A solid is one kind of matter. Like all matter, it takes up space and has mass. A **solid** is the only form of matter that has a shape of its own.

Finding Out About Solids

All the objects you see here are solids. They are different in color, size, and shape. They have different textures. A texture is the way something feels.

Solids are alike in some important ways. Each one has its own size and shape. A solid will not change in size or shape unless you do something such as cut, bend, or break it.

■ **How are these objects alike and different?**

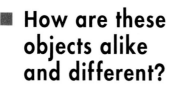

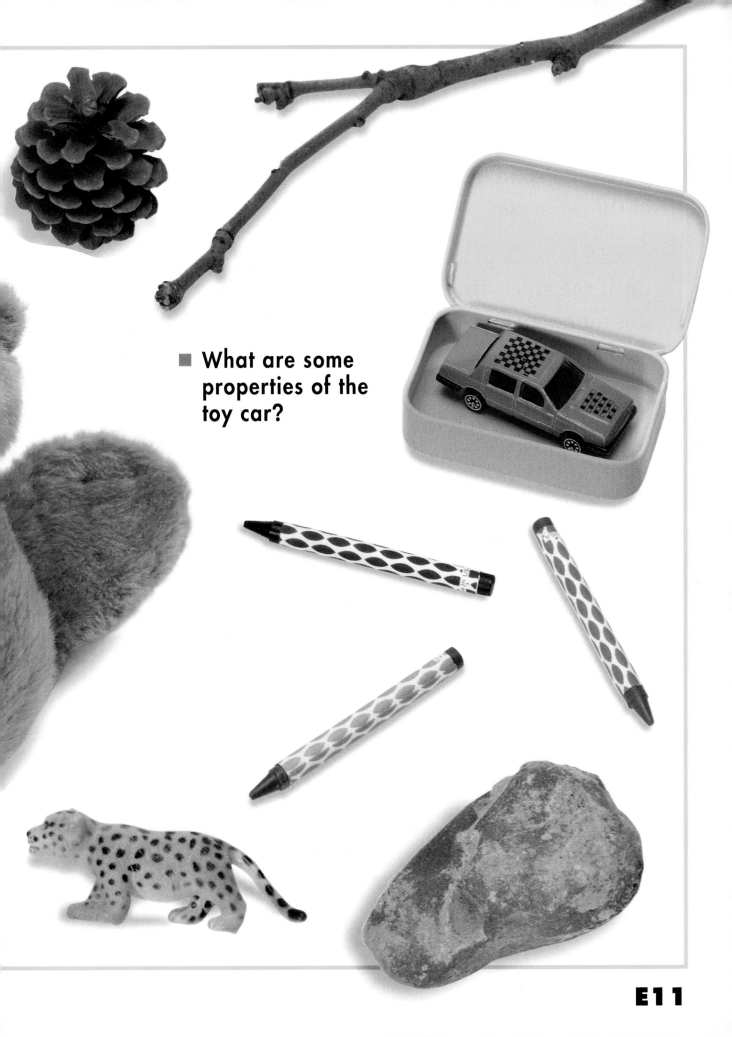

■ What are some properties of the toy car?

Measuring Solids

A balance can help you find out the mass of a solid. Put the solid on one side of the balance.

Add masses to the other side until the sides are even. There are numbers on the masses. Add them to find how much mass equals the mass of the solid.

■ **What is this girl using to measure the mass of the toy?**

You can measure how long or wide a solid is. You can also measure how big around it is.

A **centimeter** is a unit used to measure length. You can use centimeters to find the length of a solid.

centimeter

■ **What is the boy using to measure the wood?**

How Many Centimeters Long?	
Object	Number of Centimeters
box	28
wood	27

Think About It

1. How are all solids alike?

2. How can you measure the length of a solid?

What Can We Find Out About Liquids?

Liquids

You will need

marker

3 colors of water

measuring cup

3 containers

1 Draw a line at the same height on all 3 containers. Pour water into each container to the line.

2 Pour the water from one container into the measuring cup. Measure, and record the number on the cup.

3 Repeat Step 2 for the other containers.

4 Compare the numbers. What can you infer?

Science Skill

You can use a measuring cup to measure the amount of a liquid.

Liquids

A **liquid** is a form of matter that does not have its own shape. It flows to take the shape of its container. Like a solid, a liquid takes up space and has mass. You can see and feel a liquid.

Finding Out About Liquids

The liquid in a bottle has the same shape as the bottle. As you tilt the bottle, the liquid changes shape. If the liquid is poured from the bottle into a glass, it takes the shape of the glass.

■ **What shape has the honey taken?**

A liquid does not change in amount unless you add more or take some away. If you pour it into a glass, the amount of liquid stays the same.

■ **How has the shape of the lemonade changed here?**

Measuring Liquids

Like solids, liquids have mass. A container with liquid in it has more mass than the same container with no liquid. You can measure the mass of a liquid by putting it on a pan balance.

■ **Which cup has more mass? How do you know?**

You can also measure the volume of a liquid. Volume is the amount of space a liquid takes up. A **milliliter** is a unit used to measure the volume of a liquid.

Volume in Milliliters	
Liquid	Number of Milliliters
apple juice	75 milliliters
orange juice	150 milliliters

Think About It

1. What are two properties of liquids?
2. How can you measure a liquid?

What Can We Find Out About Gases?

Gases

You will need

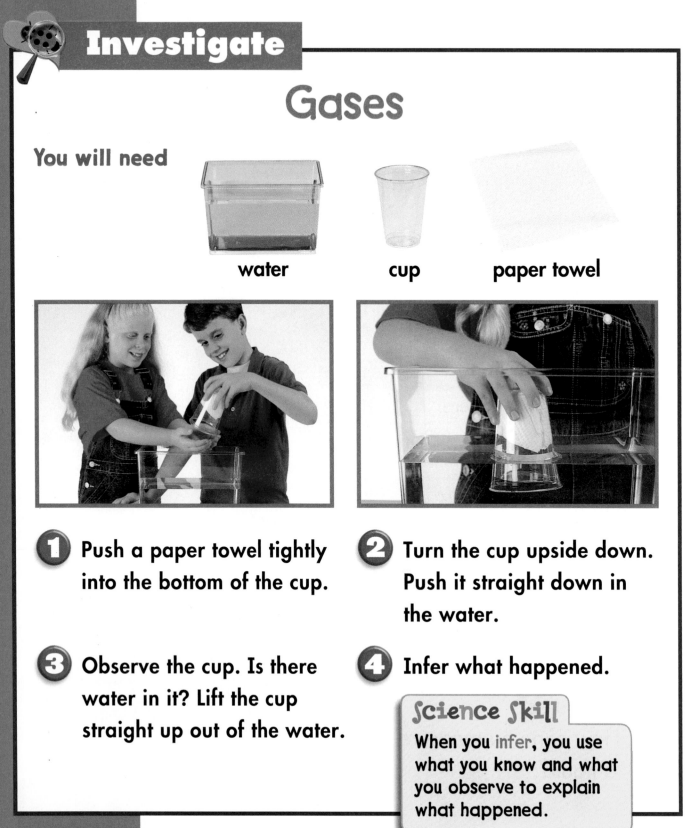

water   cup   paper towel

1 Push a paper towel tightly into the bottom of the cup.

2 Turn the cup upside down. Push it straight down in the water.

3 Observe the cup. Is there water in it? Lift the cup straight up out of the water.

4 Infer what happened.

Science Skill

When you infer, you use what you know and what you observe to explain what happened.

Gases

Like all matter, gas takes up space and has mass. Like a liquid, a gas takes the shape of its container. A **gas** is the only kind of matter that always fills all the space inside a container.

The Shapes Gases Take

When you pump air into a soccer ball, the air spreads out inside. It fills the space of its container. The air takes the round shape of the ball.

■ What shape is the air inside the bubble?

Air

Air is made up of gases and is all around you. You often cannot see or feel air, but you can see what it does. Air can lift a kite and fill a swimming float.

■ **How is this girl using air?**

Measuring Gases

Like all matter, gases have mass. You can measure the mass of a gas by tying balloons to the ends of a rod. A balloon filled with air is heavier than a balloon just like it with no air.

■ **How do you know the balloon filled with air is heavier?**

An inventor makes something new to solve a problem. Garrett Morgan was an inventor. He knew some gases were harmful. He invented a gas mask to keep firefighters and others safe from harmful gases.

gas mask

Think About It

1. What is a gas?
2. How can you measure a gas?

Math Link

Find Solid Figures

In math, figures that are not flat are called solids. Spheres, cubes, and cylinders are solid figures. A sphere has the shape of a ball. A cube has the shape of a box. A cylinder has the shape of a can. Many of the solid objects you see have these shapes.

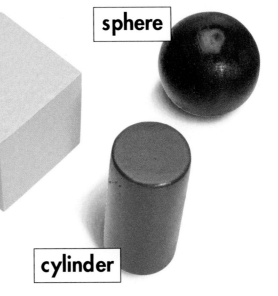

sphere

cube

cylinder

Think and Do

Make a chart. In your classroom, find objects that match the three figures. Draw a picture of each object, and write a label for it.

Solid Figures		
Sphere	Cube	Cylinder
baseball		

How Much Liquid Is in Fruit?

Many living things are partly solid and partly liquid. These fruits are solid outside, but inside them is juice—a liquid.

Think and Do

With your teacher, wash and peel fruit, and cut it into rings. Place the rings on a balance. Find and record the mass. Then trace the fruit rings.

Hang the rings in a sunny window. Predict what will happen to the mass. After 5 days, find and record the mass. Trace the dried fruit rings. Did you predict correctly?

Tell What You Know

1. What are the properties of each kind of matter?

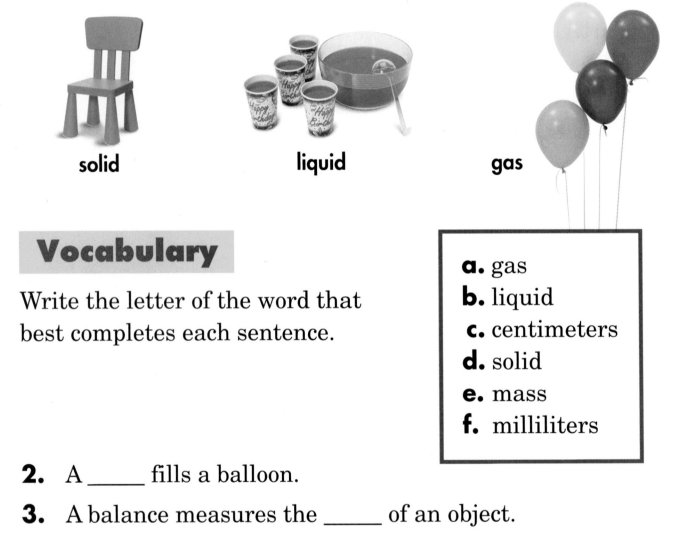

solid   liquid   gas

Vocabulary

Write the letter of the word that best completes each sentence.

> **a.** gas
> **b.** liquid
> **c.** centimeters
> **d.** solid
> **e.** mass
> **f.** milliliters

2. A _____ fills a balloon.

3. A balance measures the _____ of an object.

4. A _____ takes the shape of a bottle.

5. Liquids may be measured in _____ .

6. An object's length may be measured in _____ .

7. A chair is a _____ because it keeps its shape.

Using Science Skills

8. **Classify** Make a chart like this one. Then look through old magazines to find pictures that show each kind of matter. Cut out the pictures and glue them in the correct places. Write a label for each picture.

Kinds of Matter		
Solids	Liquids	Gases

9. **Measure** Choose five small objects to measure. With a centimeter ruler, measure them and record how long each object is. Then put the objects in order from shortest to longest.

CHAPTER 2
Changes in Matter

Vocabulary

mixture
reversible
irreversible

Did You Know?

Mixing salt and water is **reversible**. When some of the water in the Great Salt Lake dries up, the salt separates from the water.

Air is a **mixture** of 11 different gases.

What Happens When You Mix Matter?

Investigate

Mixing Matter

You will need

plastic knife

nuts, seeds, dried fruit

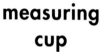

measuring cup

zip-top bag

1 Cut up the dried fruit. Measure 100 milliliters each of nuts, seeds, and fruit.

2 Put the foods in the bag. Close the bag tightly and shake.

3 Observe. What has changed or not changed?

Science Skill
You can use more than one of your senses to observe something changing.

Cutting and Mixing Matter

Matter can be cut and mixed. When solid matter is cut, its shape changes, but its mass stays the same. When pieces of solid matter are mixed together, each piece stays the same.

E33

Cutting and Shaping Matter

Cutting is just one way you can change matter. This loaf of bread is a solid. It has been cut into slices. The slices have a different shape from the loaf, but they are the same bread. Together, the slices have the same mass as the loaf.

■ How did the paper change when it was cut? How has it stayed the same?

If you change just the shape of matter, its mass stays the same. These two pieces of clay were once alike. They had the same shape and the same mass. Then the shape of one piece was changed, but its mass is still the same.

■ **How do you know the two pieces of clay have the same mass?**

Mixing Matter

When you put different kinds of matter together, you make a mixture. A **mixture** is something made up of two or more things. Things you put together in a mixture do not change.

A taco is filled with a mixture of beans, cheese, tomatoes, sauce, and lettuce. If you separate the foods in the mixture, you will find that they have not changed. For example, the beans are still beans.

■ What foods have been mixed together to fill the taco?

■ **What kinds of things are in the jar? Why is this a mixture?**

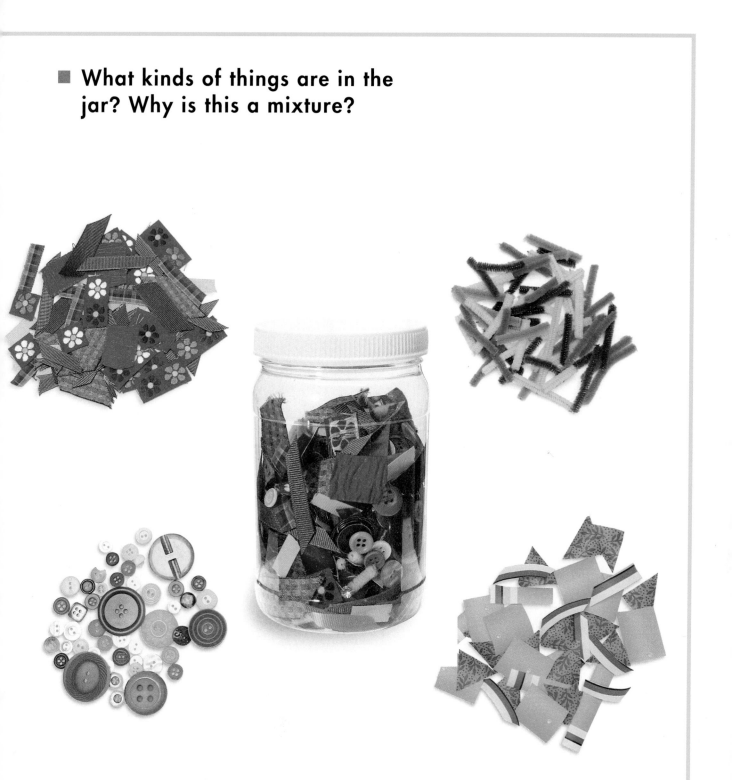

Think About It

1. What happens when you cut and shape matter?
2. What happens when you mix matter together?

How Can Water Change?

One Way That Water Changes

You will need

ice cubes

lamp

cloth

clock

1 Write about some ways to make an ice cube melt faster.

2 Plan an investigation for two of the ways. Follow your plan.

CAUTION Be careful if you use the lamp.

3 Record the time it takes each ice cube to melt.

4 Communicate to a classmate which way melted the ice faster.

Science Skill
You can plan an investigation to see which way works the best.

How Water Can Change

Water can be a solid, a gas, or a liquid. Water as a solid may be ice or snow. Water as a gas is water vapor. In this picture, heat from the Earth is changing water from one form to another.

geysers,
Yellowstone National Park

Adding Heat Changes Water

Adding heat can make water change from one form of matter to another. Ice is water in its solid form. Water is a solid only when its temperature is 0°C or lower.

Adding heat raises the temperature of the ice. If the temperature goes above 0°C, the ice melts, or changes to a liquid.

■ **Why are the icicles melting?**

A puddle is liquid water. The sun's heat may cause the water in the puddle to evaporate, or change to water vapor.

When water gets hot enough, it boils, like the water in a kettle. When water boils, it evaporates.

■ **What makes liquid water turn into a gas?**

Taking Away Heat Changes Water

Taking away heat, or cooling, can also change the form of water. When enough heat is taken away from water, it freezes, or becomes a solid called ice. When enough heat is taken away from water vapor, it condenses, or becomes liquid. Drops of liquid water form clouds and may fall as rain.

■ **How did the cloud form?**

Rain collects in lakes as liquid water. When the weather gets cold, the water freezes, or changes to ice. When the weather gets warm, the ice melts, or changes to liquid water.

■ **How did the water in this lake change?**

Water changes from liquid to ice and back, and from liquid to vapor and back. All these changes are reversible. In a **reversible** change, matter can be changed back to the way it was.

Think About It

1. What are the three forms of water?

2. What can make water change its form?

What Other Ways Does Matter Change?

A Mixture

You will need

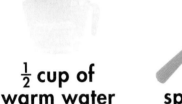

$\frac{1}{2}$ cup of warm water

spoon

salt

pan

1 Mix one spoonful of salt into the water. Stir well.

2 Pour the salt and water mixture into the pan.

3 Put the pan in a warm place. Predict what will happen.

4 Observe in two days. Did you predict correctly?

Science Skill

When you predict, you use what you know to make a good guess.

Other Ways Matter Changes

Matter can change in different ways. Some changes are reversible. Other changes are not reversible. How has the matter in this pizza changed?

Mixing and Shaping

You can mix together some things and then separate them again. Each thing will still be the same as it was before.

■ **Why is this mixture reversible?**

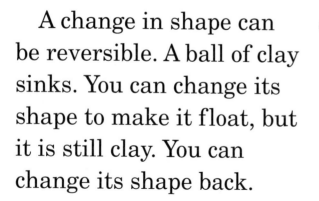

A change in shape can be reversible. A ball of clay sinks. You can change its shape to make it float, but it is still clay. You can change its shape back.

Gelatin must be changed before it is ready to eat. First, the solid powder is mixed with hot water. When the hot liquid mixture cools, it becomes firm. If the gelatin is heated, it begins to change back. Some of the gelatin melts and becomes liquid again.

■ How can a gelatin dessert change?

Burning and Cooking

Some changes to matter are **irreversible**, or not able to change back. In an irreversible change, matter cannot be changed back to the way it once was. Fire and high heat often cause irreversible changes.

Burning causes wood to change to ashes and smoke. The ashes, gases, and smoke cannot be changed back to wood again.

■ What irreversible change will this fire cause?

Cooking can also cause irreversible changes. Cooking makes an egg change from a liquid to a solid. It also makes the egg change in color, texture, and taste. You cannot do anything to make the cooked egg become raw, or uncooked, again.

■ **How did the egg change?**

Think About It

1. What are some changes in matter that are reversible?
2. What are some changes in matter that are irreversible?

Math Link

How Much Liquid Changes to a Gas?

You can use a measuring cup to find out how much liquid water changes into a gas.

Think and Do

Pour 100 mL of water into a measuring cup. Put the cup on a windowsill in the sun.

After three days, measure and record how much water is in the cup. Write a subtraction problem to figure out how much of the water evaporated, or changed to a gas.

Art Link

A Potter Changes the Shape of Matter

A potter uses clay to make beautiful things. This potter is shaping clay into a pot. He will put the clay pot in a special oven. The clay will change to a different kind of matter that is very hard. Some kinds of clay can get hard just by drying in the air.

Think and Do

Make a pot from clay. Work the clay into a shape. Try using different colors of clay to make your pot more interesting.

REVIEW

Tell What You Know

1. Tell how matter is being changed in each picture.

Vocabulary

Tell which pictures answer the questions.

a.

2. Which picture shows an *irreversible* change?

3. Which picture shows a *mixture*?

b.

4. Which picture shows a *reversible* change?

c.

Using Science Skills

5. **Plan and Conduct a Simple Investigation/Predict** Plan a way to show how water can change from a liquid to a solid and back to a liquid. List the materials you will need. Draw pictures to show each step you will take. Predict what will happen, and then follow your plan. Did you predict correctly?

6. **Observe/Classify** Look at pictures in magazines. Find three kinds of foods that are mixtures. Then make a chart like this one. Write the name of each mixture. Then list the foods that make up each one.

Food Mixtures		
Mixture 1 _____	Mixture 2 _____	Mixture 3 _____

The Strength of Air

1. Close a zip-top bag around a straw. Then blow into the straw.

2. Pull out the straw, and quickly finish zipping the bag closed.

3. How many books can you pile on your bag of air? Record what you observe.

4. Does air take up space? Can the air in the bag hold a lot of books? Share what you observe.

Disappearing Water

1. Pour the same amount of water into two clear cups that are the same size and shape.

2. Use tape to mark the level of water in each cup.

3. Cover one cup with plastic wrap.

4. Leave the cups side-by-side for a few days.

5. Write about what you observe. What happens to the water in the two cups? Why?

Make Saltwater Pictures

1. With an adult, mix salt in a cup of very warm water.

2. Use a toothpick to make a design with the salt water on black paper.

3. Let the paper dry all night.

4. Describe what happened to the water. Tell what happened to the salt.

Grow Rock Candy

1. Have an adult help you mix a lot of sugar in a cup of very warm water.

2. Tie one end of a string to the middle of a craft stick.

3. Lay the stick across the mouth of the cup with the string hanging down.

4. Cut the string so that it just touches the bottom of the cup.

5. Observe the string every day for a week or more. Record what happens.

WRITING

Recipe Cards Think of a food you would like to make that mixes or changes matter. Write steps to make that food.

READING

Puddle Jumper: How a Toy Is Made
by Ann Morris
How does a toymaker change matter to make a moving toy? Talk about what you learn.

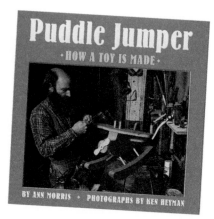

COMPUTER CENTER
Visit *The Learning Site* at
www.harcourtschool.com

Energy in Motion

Physical Science

Energy in Motion

UNIT PROJECT

Parade Time!

Plan a parade. Make floats that move. Put sounds together for a marching band.

Forces and Motion

Vocabulary

force
location
wind
gravity
motion

Did You Know?
Cheetahs use **motion** to catch their food. They are the fastest land animals.

Did You Know?

Sometimes **wind** is so strong it can push a piece of wood through a roof.

What Are Forces?

 Investigate

Pushes and Pulls

You will need

paper and pencil

Pushes and Pulls		
What I Moved	Push	Pull

1 Make a chart like this one.

2 Move some objects. Observe how you move them.

3 Ask yourself if you used a push or a pull to move each object. Record your answers.

4 Share with a classmate what you observed.

Science Skill
When you move objects, you can observe pushes and pulls.

Forces

A **force** is a push or a pull that makes something move. These children are trying to get the dog to move. Which child is pushing? Which child is pulling?

Pushes and Pulls

You can push or pull something to change its location. A **location** is the place where something is. You can also use a push or a pull to stop something from moving.

You use forces to open a can. You push on the can opener to make it turn. The can opener pulls the can around.

You use forces to change the direction of a moving object. When you push a ball, you change its location. If the ball is moving, your push also changes the direction it is moving in.

■ **Which kind of force is this dog using?**

Kinds of Forces

Moving air is a force called **wind**. The wind pushes on the sails of a sailboat to make the boat move.

Moving water is also a force that moves things. You can see and feel the force of water in rivers, streams, and oceans.

■ **How is water moving the raft?**

The force that pulls things toward the center of Earth is called **gravity**. A sled moves down a hill because of gravity. Gravity keeps us on the ground.

Magnetism is also a force. You can use a magnet to pull objects made of iron. Magnets can move iron objects without touching them.

■ **What force is the boy using to make the picture?**

Think About It

1. What is a force?

2. How can you use forces?

How Can We Measure Motion?

One Way to Measure Motion

You will need

board

6 books

meterstick

toy truck

1. Make a low ramp. Let the toy truck roll down.

2. Measure from the bottom of the ramp to where the truck stopped. Record the distance.

3. Make the ramp higher. Then repeat Steps 1 and 2.

4. Use numbers to compare your data. When did the truck go farther? Why?

Science Skill

You can use numbers to find out how far an object moves.

Measuring Motion

Forces can make people and things move. When something moves, it is in **motion**. These people are in motion. What force is making them move?

Force and Motion

Something light is easier to move than something heavy. Less force is needed to move light things, and more force is needed to move heavy things.

It also takes less force to move something on a smooth surface than on a rough surface. It takes less force to pull a wagon on a sidewalk than on grass. A rough surface like grass causes more friction. Friction is a force that makes it harder to move things.

It takes less force to move something a short distance than a long distance. To move a ball a short distance, you kick it gently. To move it farther, you kick it hard.

■ **In which picture will the ball go farther? Why?**

Ways to Measure Motion

You can measure how far an object or a person moves. In a jumping contest, you try to jump as far as you can. Someone measures how far you jump.

What tool is being used to measure how far the girl jumps?

You can also measure how much time something or someone takes to move from one place to another. In a race, a timekeeper measures how much time racers take to reach the finish line.

You can use a rubber band to measure how much force it takes to move something. The rubber band stretches less when you pull with less force. It stretches more when you pull with more force.

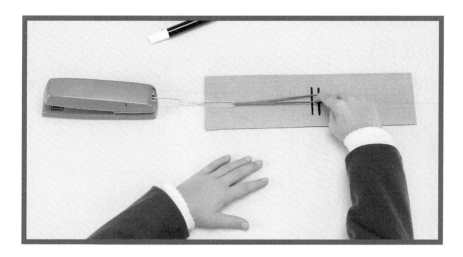

■ **Which picture shows more force being used?**

Think About It

1. What makes things move?

2. How can you measure motion?

Math/Literature Link

The Enormous Turnip

The folktale *The Enormous Turnip* is about a turnip so big that a man cannot pull it up. How will the man and his family pull up the turnip? You can read the book to find out how much force it takes.

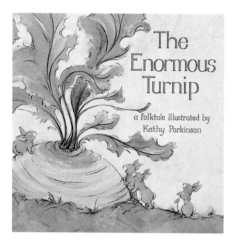

The Enormous Turnip

a folktale illustrated by Kathy Parkinson

Think and Do

See how much force it takes to move things. Tie a book to a spring scale. Pull on the spring scale. As the book moves, read the numbers on the scale. Repeat with other objects, and compare the numbers. Which object needs the most force to be moved?

A Personal Trainer

A personal trainer teaches people how to exercise the right way. This personal trainer is showing a woman how to use a weight machine. The bar of this machine connects to weights. The woman must pull down and push up on the bar to move the weights.

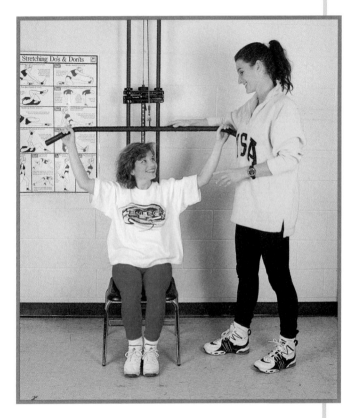

Think and Do

Think of some exercises you know how to do. As you do each one, observe when you are pushing or pulling. Then show a classmate how to do the exercises. Use the words *push* and *pull.*

Tell What You Know

Tell which picture answers each question.

a. b. c. d. e.

1. How can gravity change an object's location?

2. How can you measure how far a thing moves?

3. How can you measure how long someone takes to move from one place to another?

4. How can a push change an object's direction?

5. Which is a pull?

Vocabulary

6. Use these words to tell about the picture.

  force   location

  gravity   motion

Using Science Skills

7. **Observe** Make a chart like this one, and then observe objects in motion. Was it a push or a pull? Write whether a *push* or a *pull* moves each object.

Which Forces Move Objects?				
Object	Wind	Water	Gravity	Other
Boat	push	push		

8. **Use Numbers** Make a ramp like this one. Place a toy car at the top, and let it go. Measure how far the car travels. Then cover the ramp with a thick towel and try again. When does the car travel farther? faster?

Try two other surfaces. Use numbers to measure each distance, and compare.

CHAPTER 2

Sound

Vocabulary

sound
vibrate
loudness
pitch
sonar
music

Did You Know?

Elephants can make and hear sounds that are so low in **pitch** that humans can't hear them.

Did You Know?

Crickets hear **sound** through ears on their legs.

ear

What Is Sound?

What Makes Sound

You will need

ruler   paper and pencil

1 Hold the ruler on a desk so one end hangs over the edge. Push that end down and let it go.

2 Observe and record what happens.

3 How could you change the sound? Plan an investigation.

4 Follow your plan. Tell a classmate what you find out.

Science Skill
When you plan an investigation, you ask a question and test ways to answer the question.

What Makes Sound

The energy that lets you hear is **sound**.
Sound is made when things **vibrate**, or move
back and forth very fast.

Sound and Air

When something vibrates, it makes the air around it vibrate, too. The strings of a guitar vibrate when you pluck them. The vibrations travel through the air to your ears. Then you hear the sound the guitar makes.

Sound moves through the air in every direction. When a school bell rings, people all around the bell can hear it.

Sound can also be blocked. Some people who work near loud machines wear ear coverings. The coverings block some of the sound vibrations from reaching their ears.

■ **Why did this person cover his ears?**

How You Hear Sounds

You hear sounds with your ears. Sound vibrations move through the air into each ear. The vibrations reach your eardrum and make it vibrate.

eardrum

How You Make Sounds

You use your vocal cords to make sounds in your throat. Put your hand on your throat when you talk, and you can feel the vocal cords vibrate.

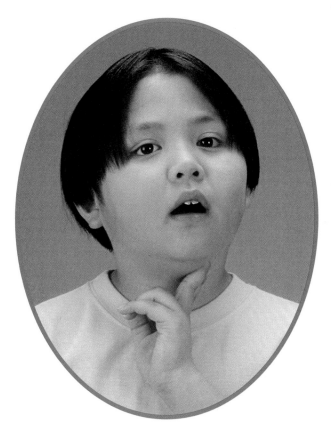

Think About It

1. What makes sound?
2. How do you hear sounds?

An audiologist tests people's hearing with machines that make sounds. An audiologist also helps people who do not hear well. You should get your hearing checked by an audiologist from time to time.

■ **What is this audiologist doing?**

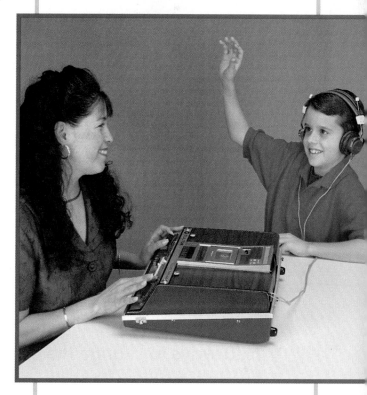

How Do Sounds Vary?

Different Sounds

You will need

3 glasses   water   spoon   paper and pencil

1 Pour a different amount of water into each glass.

2 Tap the side of each glass with the spoon.

3 Listen to the sounds. Record what you observe.

4 Find ways to change the sounds. Observe and record.

Science Skill
Listening is one way to observe.

How Sounds Can Be Different

Sounds are all around you. What sounds do you think the children in the picture hear? What sounds can you hear in your classroom?

Loud and Soft

Sounds are different in **loudness**, or how loud or soft they are. Some sounds, like yells, are loud. Other sounds, like whispers, are soft. It takes less energy to make a soft sound than a loud sound.

■ What do you do to make a loud sound?

High and Low

Sounds are also different in **pitch**, or how high or low they are. A sparrow's song is a high sound. A bullfrog's croak is a low sound.

■ How are the sounds a sparrow and a bullfrog make different?

Think About It

1. What are some loud sounds and some soft sounds?
2. What are some high sounds and some low sounds?

How Does Sound Travel?

How Sound Travels

You will need

meterstick

tape

paper and pencil

1 Measure 50 centimeters on your desk. Mark each end with tape.

2 Scratch one tape mark, and listen at the other end. Record what you hear.

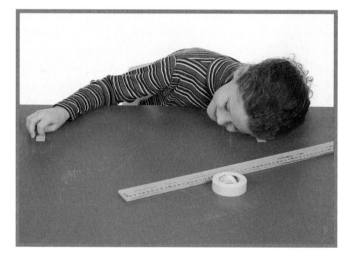

3 Predict the loudness of the sound if you put your ear on the desk. Record what you predict.

4 Try it. What do you observe? Did you predict correctly?

Science Skill

To predict, think about what you already know and then say what you think will happen.

How Sound Travels

Sound can travel through different kinds of matter. These children have their ears under water. They can still hear the coach's voice. What kinds of matter are the sounds traveling through?

Sounds Travel Through Gases and Solids

Sounds can travel through gases such as air. The sound from the vibrating bells on some alarm clocks travels through the air. It reaches a person's ears and wakes the person up.

■ **What does the sound from the horn travel through?**

Sounds can also travel through solid objects. You may have played with a string telephone. A person talks into one cup, making the air inside it vibrate. The air makes the cup vibrate, and the cup makes the string vibrate.

The vibrations travel through the string and make the other cup vibrate. That cup makes the air inside it vibrate. The vibrations travel into the other person's ear, and that person hears the sound.

■ **What vibrates when a person talks into the cup?**

Sound Travels Through Liquids

Sounds can travel through liquids, such as water. Dolphins have a kind of **sonar**, or a way to use sounds to locate objects under water. The sounds make echoes when they hit objects. The dolphins locate the objects by listening to the echoes.

dolphins

Humpback whales also make sounds under water. The sounds they make are like songs. The songs can travel a long way through the water to other whales.

■ **What do you think this whale is communicating to her young?**

humpback whales

Think About It

1. How do sounds travel?
2. What can sounds travel through?

How Can We Make Different Sounds?

Making Different Sounds

You will need

rubber bands

box lid

pencil

1 Stretch 3 rubber bands around the box lid.

2 Pluck the rubber bands. Compare the sounds.

3 Put the pencil under the rubber bands and pluck them again. Compare.

4 How did the sounds change? How did they stay the same?

Science Skill

When you compare, you look for ways that two or more things are alike and different.

How to Make Different Sounds

People use sounds to make **music**, or a combination of sounds that people enjoy. These people are playing different musical instruments. Each instrument makes a different kind of sound.

Making Different Sounds

Some musical instruments have strings. Thin strings vibrate faster and make higher sounds. Thick strings vibrate more slowly and make lower sounds.

Changing the length of a string changes how fast it vibrates. Shortening a string makes it vibrate faster and sound higher. Making the string longer makes it vibrate more slowly and sound lower.

You can change the loudness of a sound. If you use a lot of energy and hit a drum hard, it makes a loud sound. If you use just a little energy and tap the drum lightly, it makes a soft sound.

■ **How can you make different sounds with these instruments?**

Think About It

1. How can you make high sounds and low sounds?
2. How can you make loud sounds and soft sounds?

Math Link

How Long Does a Sound Last?

This musical instrument is called a triangle. When a player taps the triangle, it makes a ringing sound.

Think and Do

Tap a triangle gently. Count slowly to time how long you can hear the sound. Then hit the triangle harder. Count at the same speed to time how long you can hear this sound.

Which sound lasts longer? Write a subtraction problem to show how much longer it lasted.

Make Musical Instruments

Musical instruments can be grouped by the way they make sounds. Percussion instruments make sounds when you shake or hit them. Stringed instruments make sounds when you pluck their strings. Wind instruments make sounds when you blow into them.

percussion   stringed   wind

Think and Do

Make a musical instrument of your own. Then show a classmate how it works. Tell if it is a wind, a stringed, or a percussion instrument.

Tell What You Know

Answer the question about each picture.

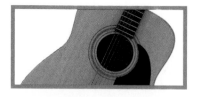

1. What vibrates to make the sound?

2. How can you change this sound?

3. How are these sounds different?

Vocabulary

Use each word to tell about a picture.

4. sonar

5. music

6. pitch

a.

b.

c.

Using Science Skills

7. Observe/Compare Make a chart like this one. Then listen for different sounds. Write the information in your chart.

Kinds of Sounds		
Sound Maker	High or Low	Loud or Soft

8. Plan an Investigation/Compare Investigate how to change the pitch of a sound. Blow into an empty bottle. Listen to the sound. Now think of ways to change its pitch. Try out your ideas.

Push or Pull Toys?

1. Observe some toys. Do you push them or pull them or both?

2. Make a chart to classify the toys as toys you push, toys you pull, or both.

3. Use your chart to help you communicate to classmates what you observe.

Magnetic Puppet Show

1. Draw puppets on cardboard. Cut them out.

2. Bend the bottom of the puppet back to make a tab. Tape a paper clip onto the tab.

3. Cut off one side of a box to make a stage.

4. Place the puppets on the stage.

5. Use magnets under the stage to move the puppets around.

Make Chicken Sounds

1. Punch two holes in the bottom of a paper cup.

2. Push a string through the holes and tie a knot.

3. Wet the string. Move your fingers along the string in short, jerky movements.

4. Tell what sounds you hear and how they are made.

Play a Listening Game

1. All players but the one who is "it" close their eyes.

2. The player who is "it" makes a sound.

3. The other players guess how the sound is being made. They may need clues from the player who is "it."

4. The first player to guess correctly makes the next sound.

★Announcement★
The science
fair is
today at
3 p.m.
Meet in the
auditorium.

WRITING

Sound Off Write an announcement about something happening at school. Make a paper megaphone or another tool to share your message.

READING

Sounds All Around
by Wendy Pfeffer
What kinds of sounds are around us every day? Read this book to find out.

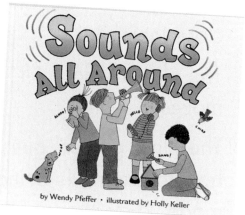

COMPUTER CENTER
Visit *The Learning Site* at
www.harcourtschool.com

References

Investigating

This plan will help you work like a scientist.

STEP 1 — Ask a question.

Which paper towel will be the strongest when wet?

STEP 2 — Make a prediction.

I predict this paper towel will be the strongest.

STEP 3 — Plan a fair test.

I will put each paper towel in water. Then I will put the same block on each towel to test it.

STEP 4 — Do your test.

I'll record what happens to each towel.

STEP 5 — Draw a conclusion.

My prediction was correct! This paper towel was the strongest.

Investigate More

Which paper towel will hold the most water?

Using Science Tools

Hand Lens

A hand lens makes things look larger than they are.

1. Hold the hand lens close to your face.
2. Move the object until you see it clearly.

Thermometer

Scientists use the Celsius scale on a thermometer to measure temperature.

1. Place the thermometer in the liquid.
2. Wait about two minutes.
3. Find the line that meets the top of the liquid.
4. Read the number. This is the temperature.

The temperature is 40°C.

This leaf is 21 centimeters long.

Ruler

A ruler is a tool that lets you measure how long something is.

1. Put the edge of the ruler at the end of the object.
2. Read the number at the other end.

Meterstick

A meterstick is a tool that lets you measure in centimeters.

1. Put the beginning edge of the meterstick at the beginning point.
2. Read the number at the other end to measure the distance.

This paper is 30 centimeters long.

Measuring Cup

Use a measuring cup to measure how much liquid there is.

1. Pour the liquid into the cup.
2. Put the cup on a table.
3. Wait until the liquid is still.
4. Look at the level of the liquid.
5. Read how much liquid is in the cup.

There are 350 milliliters of liquid here.

Clock

A clock lets you measure time. Some clocks have a minute hand and an hour hand.

1. Look at the hour hand.
2. Look at the minute hand.
3. Read the time.

It is 11:30.

Stopwatch

A stopwatch measures how much time passes.

1. To start timing, press START.
2. To stop timing, press STOP.
3. Read how much time has passed.

Twenty-five seconds have gone by.

Balance

Use a balance to measure the mass of an object.

1. Make the pans even.
2. Put the object in one pan.
3. Add masses to the other pan until the pans are even again.
4. Count up the number of masses. The total is the mass of the object.

Computer

Computers are tools, too. Here are some ways a computer can help you.

1. Some computers help you draw or make charts.
2. Most computers help you find answers to questions.
3. Many computers help you communicate. This can mean writing, sending, or receiving information.

Measurements

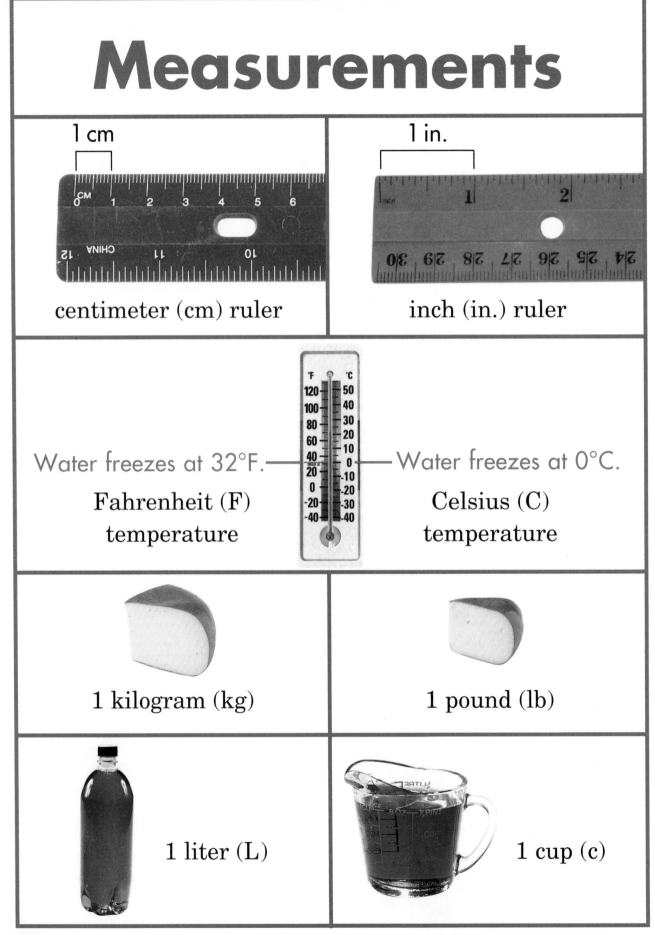

1 cm

centimeter (cm) ruler

1 in.

inch (in.) ruler

Water freezes at 32°F.

Fahrenheit (F)
temperature

Water freezes at 0°C.

Celsius (C)
temperature

1 kilogram (kg)

1 pound (lb)

1 liter (L)

1 cup (c)

Health Handbook

Getting Exercise

Warm-Up and Cool-Down Stretches

Warm up your muscles before you exercise. Spend at least five minutes stretching. You can use any of the stretches shown here. Hold each stretch while you count to 15. Repeat each stretch three times. Remember to start exercising slowly.

Slow down at the end of exercise. Then repeat some of these stretches for about two minutes. Stretching after exercise helps your muscles cool down.

▼ **Shoulder and Chest Stretch** Pull your hands slowly toward the floor. Keep your elbows straight, but don't lock them.

▶ **Sit-and-Reach Stretch** Bend forward at the waist. Keep your eyes on your toes.

◀ **Calf Stretch** Keep both feet on the floor. Try changing the distance between your feet. Where do you get a better stretch?

▲ **Upper Back and Shoulder Stretch**
Try to stretch your hand down so
that it rests flat against your back.

▼ **Thigh Stretch** Keep both hands
flat on the ground. Lean as far
forward as you can.

▲ **Leg Stretch**
Extend one leg
behind you. Keep
the toes of that
foot pointed up.

Tips for Stretching

- Never bounce. Stretch gently.
- Breathe normally to get the air you need.
- Never stretch until it hurts. You should
  feel only a slight pull.

Getting Exercise

Build Your Heart and Lungs

Exercise helps your heart and lungs grow strong. The best exercise activities make you breathe deeply. They make your heart beat fast. You should try to exercise for at least twenty minutes at a time. Remember to warm up first and cool down at the end.

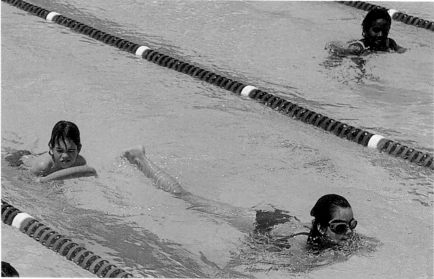

▲ **Swimming** If you are not a strong swimmer, use a kickboard to get a good workout. Remember to swim only when a lifeguard is present.

◄ **Skating** Always wear a helmet, elbow and knee pads, wrist guards, and gloves. Learn to skate, stop, and fall correctly.

▼ **Riding a Bike** When you ride your bike, your exercise really gets you somewhere! Follow bike safety rules, and always wear your helmet.

▶ **Walking** A fast walk can help build your heart and lungs. Wear shoes that support your feet. Walk with a friend for extra fun!

▶ **Jumping Rope** Jumping rope is good for your heart and your lungs. Always jump on a flat surface. Wear shoes that support your feet.

Staying Safe

Fire Safety

You can stay safe from fires. Follow these safety rules.

- Never play with matches or lighters.
- Be careful around stoves, heaters, fireplaces, and grills.
- Don't use microwaves, irons, or toasters without an adult's help.
- Practice your family's fire safety plan.
- If there is a fire in your home, get out quickly. Drop to the floor and crawl if the room is filled with smoke. If a closed door feels hot, don't open it. Use another exit. Call 911 from outside your home.
- If your clothes catch on fire, use Stop, Drop, and Roll right away to put out the flames.

❶ **Stop** Don't run or wave your arms.

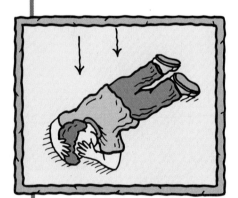

❷ **Drop** Lie down quickly. Cover your eyes with your hands.

❸ **Roll** Roll back and forth to put out the fire.

Stranger Danger

You can stay safe around strangers.
Follow these rules.

- Never talk to strangers.
- Never go with a stranger, on foot or in a car.
- If you are home alone, do not open the door. Do not let telephone callers know you are alone.
- Never give your name, address, or phone number to anyone you don't know. (You may give this information to a 911 operator in an emergency.)
- If you are lost or need help, talk to a police officer, a guard, or a store clerk.
- If a stranger bothers you, use the Stranger Danger rules to stay safe.

❶ **Say no!** Yell if you need to. You do not have to be polite to strangers.

❷ **Get away.** Walk fast or run in the opposite direction. Go toward people who can help you.

❸ **Tell someone.** Tell a trusted adult, such as a family member, a teacher, or a police officer. Do not keep secrets about strangers.

Bike Safety

A Safe Bike

To ride your bike safely, you need to start with a safe bike. A safe bike is the right size for you. When you sit on your bike with the pedal in the lowest position, you should be able to rest your heel on the pedal.

After checking the size of your bike, check to see that it has the right safety equipment. Your bike should have everything shown below.

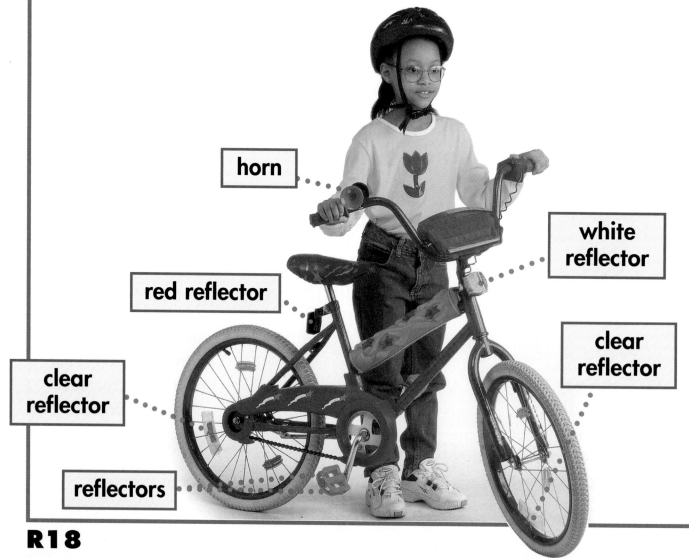

horn

white reflector

red reflector

clear reflector

clear reflector

reflectors

Your Bike Helmet

◀ Always wear a bike helmet. Wear your helmet flat on your head. Be sure it is strapped tightly. If your helmet gets bumped in a fall, replace it right away, even if it doesn't look damaged.

Safety on the Road

- Check your bike for safety every time you ride it.
- Ride in single file. Ride in the same direction as traffic.
- Stop, look, listen, and think when you enter a street or cross a driveway.
- Walk your bike across an intersection.
- Obey all traffic signs and signals.
- Don't ride at night without an adult. Wear light-colored clothing and use lights and reflectors for night riding.

Sense Organs

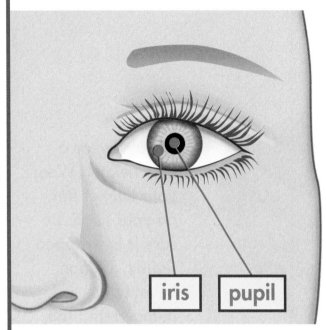

Outside of Eye

Caring for Your Eyes and Ears

- Sunglasses protect your eyes. Wear sunglasses when you are outdoors in sunlight or snow or on the water.
- Never put anything in your ears.

Eyes

Your eyes let you see. When you look at your eyes, you see a white part, a colored part, and a hole. The colored part is the iris. The hole in the middle is the pupil.

Inside of Eye

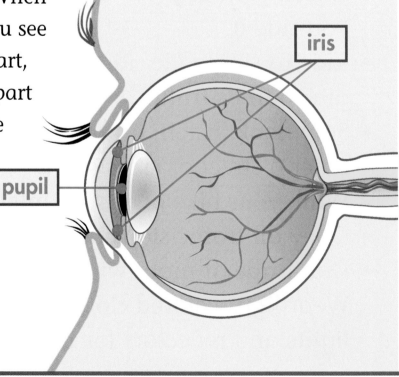

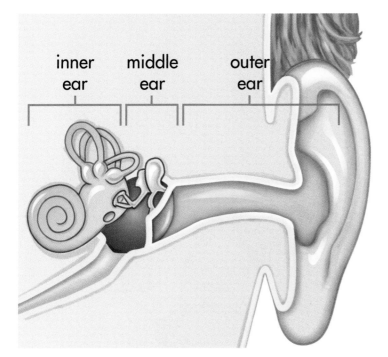

inner ear   middle ear   outer ear

Inside of Ear   **Outside of Ear**

Ears

Your ears let you hear. What you see on the outside of your head is only part of your ear. The main part of your ear is inside your head.

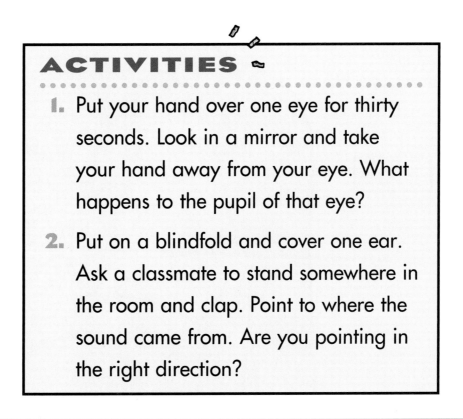

ACTIVITIES

1. Put your hand over one eye for thirty seconds. Look in a mirror and take your hand away from your eye. What happens to the pupil of that eye?

2. Put on a blindfold and cover one ear. Ask a classmate to stand somewhere in the room and clap. Point to where the sound came from. Are you pointing in the right direction?

The Respiratory System

When you breathe, you are using your respiratory system. Your mouth, your nose, your lungs, and your diaphragm are parts of your respiratory system.

Caring for Your Respiratory System

- Never put anything in your nose.

- Playing helps your lungs. When you climb and jump, you breathe harder. Breathing harder makes your lungs stronger.

nose

mouth

lungs

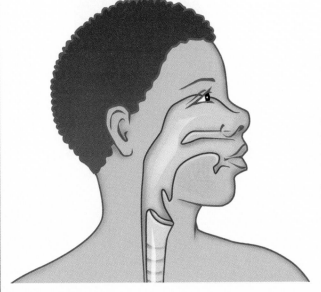

Mouth and Nose

Air goes in and out of your body through your mouth and nose. Your mouth and nose warm the air you breathe.

Lungs

You have two lungs. Your lungs are in your chest. When you breathe in, your lungs fill with air. When you breathe out, air leaves your lungs.

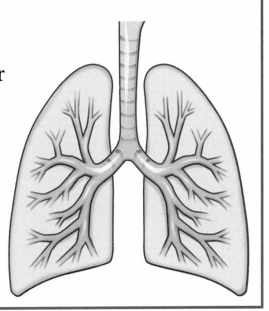

ACTIVITIES

1. Try to say something while you're breathing in. Try to say something while you're breathing out. Which is easier?

2. Breathe onto a mirror. What happens? Rinse your mouth with cold water. Again breathe on the mirror. What happens?

The Muscular System

The muscles in your body help you move. When you blink, you are using muscles. When you run, you are using muscles. Even when you eat, you are using muscles.

Caring for Your Muscular System

Stretch your muscles before you use them for play or exercise.

ACTIVITY

Wiggle your nose. Stick out your tongue. Wrinkle your forehead. Smile. Are you using muscles?

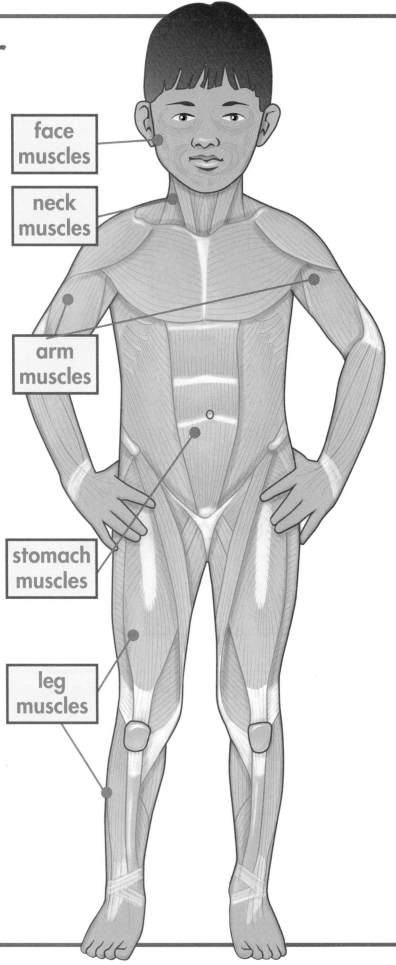

face muscles

neck muscles

arm muscles

stomach muscles

leg muscles

The Nervous System

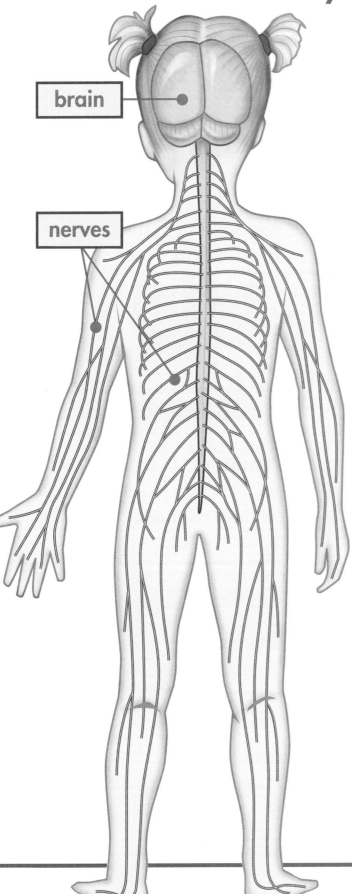

brain

nerves

Your nervous system makes your muscles work and tells you about your surroundings. Your brain and your nerves are parts of your nervous system.

Caring for Your Nervous System

Get plenty of sleep. Sleeping lets your brain rest.

ACTIVITY

Have a classmate blindfold you and fill one cup with cold water and another cup with warm water. Stick your finger in each cup. Can you tell which is the cold water and which is the warm water?

GLOSSARY

A

amphibian [am•fib′ē•ən] An animal that lives both in water and on land. A frog is an amphibian. (A27)

C

cactus [kak′təs] A plant that can store water in its thick stems. A cactus grows in the desert. (A17)

Arctic [ärk′tik] A place with a cold, windy environment where the land is covered with ice and snow for most of the year. (B13)

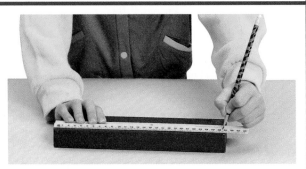

centimeter [sen′tə•mēt′ər] A unit used to measure length. A crayon is about 9 centimeters long. (E13)

B

boulder [bōl′dər] A large rock. A boulder can be larger than a person. (C6)

cirrus [sir′əs] A kind of cloud that is thin, feathery, and high in the sky. We see cirrus clouds in sunny weather. (D48)

constellation
[kän′stə•lā′shən] A group of stars that form a star picture. The Big Dipper is a constellation. (D26)

D

desert [dez′ərt] An environment that gets little rain. Only a few kinds of plants and animals live in the desert. (B10)

crater [krā′tər] A hole that has the shape of a bowl. The moon has craters. (D18)

digest [di′jest′] To break down food in the body. It is harder to digest an apple than apple juice. (A61)

cumulus [kyo͞o′myo͞o•ləs] A kind of cloud that looks like puffy white cotton. We see cumulus clouds in fair weather. (D49)

dinosaur [di′nə•sôr′] An animal that lived millions of years ago. Tyrannosaurus rex was a dinosaur. (C37)

drought [drout] A long time without rain. Many plants die during a drought. (B34)

evaporate [ē•vap′ə•rāt′] To change into a gas. Water in a puddle will evaporate in the warm sun. (D42)

E

energy [en′ər•jē] Something that can cause change and do work. Light and heat are kinds of energy. (D6)

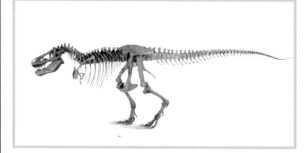

extinct [ek•stingkt′] No longer living. Because dinosaurs do not live anymore, they are extinct. (C37)

environment [en•vī′rən•mənt] All the living and nonliving things in a place. A forest is a land environment. (B5)

F

food chain [fōod′ chān′] The order in which animals eat plants and other animals. (B24)

force   [fôrs] A push or a pull that makes something move. Magnetism is one kind of force. (F5)

germinate   [jûr′mə•nāt′] To start to grow. A seed may germinate if it gets water and warmth. (A10)

fossil   [fäs′əl] What is left of a plant or an animal that lived long ago. A fossil can be a print of an animal's bones. (C27)

gravity   [grav′i•tē] A force that pulls things toward the center of Earth. Earth's gravity is stronger than the moon's. (F9)

G

gas   [gas] The only kind of matter that always fills all the space inside a container. Balloons are filled with a gas. (E21)

H

habitat   [hab′i•tat′] A place where an animal finds the things it needs to live. In its habitat this animal finds water. (B6)

heart [härt] A muscle that pumps blood to every part of the body. Your heart is the size of your fist. (A55)

irreversible [ir′ri•vûr′sə•bəl] Not able to be changed back. A cooked egg is an irreversible change. (E48)

heart rate [härt rāt] How fast or slowly a heart beats. Exercise makes a heart rate faster. (A56)

L

life cycle [līf′ sī′kəl] All the parts of an animal's life from birth to death. The life cycle of a bird has different stages. (A31)

I

insect [in′sekt′] An animal that has three body parts and six legs. Ants and bees are each a kind of insect. (A28)

liquid [lik′wid] A form of matter that does not have its own shape. Water, milk, juice, and gasoline are each a liquid. (E15)

litter [lit'ər] Trash that is not put in a trash can. Plants and animals are hurt by litter. (B40)

loudness [loud'nes] How loud or soft a sound is. A sound's loudness depends on the amount of energy used to make the sound. (F30)

living [liv'ing] Growing and changing. Plants and animals are living things because they need food, water, and air. (A5)

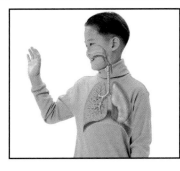

lungs [lungz] Body parts that help you breathe the air you need to live. When you breathe in, air moves into your lungs. (A55)

location [lō•kā'shən] The place where something is. You can push or pull something to change its location. (F6)

M

mammal [mam'əl] An animal that has fur or hair. A mother mammal makes milk to feed to her young. A cat is a mammal. (A26)

mass [mas] The amount of matter an object has. Use a balance to see how much mass an object has. (E7)

mineral [min′ər•əl] One kind of nonliving thing that is found in nature. Copper and iron are each a mineral. (C18)

matter [mat′ər] What all things are made of. People, clothing, air, and water are all made of matter. (E5)

mixture [miks′chər] Something made up of two or more things that do not change. Taco filling is a mixture. (E36)

milliliter [mil′i•lēt′ər] A unit used to measure the volume of a liquid. Some measuring cups measure in milliliters. (E19)

moon [moōn] The largest object you can see in the night sky. The moon takes about one month to orbit Earth. (D17)

moonlight [mo͞on′lit′] The light from the moon. Light from the sun that bounces off the moon is called moonlight. (D17)

music [myo͞o′zik] A combination of sounds that people enjoy. You can use an instrument to make music. (F39)

motion [mō′shən] The act of moving. People, animals, and things are in motion when they move. (F11)

N

natural resource [nach′ər•əl rē′sôrs′] Something found in nature that people can use to meet their needs. Rocks are one natural resource. (C7)

muscles [mus′əlz] Body parts that move your bones and do other jobs. Your muscles work in pairs. (A51)

nonliving [nän•liv′ing] Not alive. Air, water, and rocks are nonliving things. (A5)

nutrients [nōo′trē•ənts] Minerals. Plants need nutrients from the soil to grow. (A9)

permanent teeth
[pûr′mə•nənt tēth] New adult teeth that take the place of first teeth. People have 32 permanent teeth. (A46)

orbit [ôr′bit] The path around something. Earth's orbit around the sun takes one year. (D13)

pitch [pich] How high or low a sound is. The pitch of a cat's meow is higher than the pitch of a lion's roar. (F31)

paleontologist
[pā′lē•ən•täl′ə•jəst′] A scientist who finds and studies fossils. This paleontologist studies dinosaurs. (C29)

pollution [pə•lōo•shən] Waste that harms land, water, or air. Factories and cars can make pollution. (B39)

pond [pänd] A freshwater environment. Otters, turtles, and frogs live around a pond. (B15)

reconstruct [rē′kən•strukt′] To rebuild. Scientists try to reconstruct dinosaur skeletons. (C34)

property [präp′ər•tē] A quality of something. Color, size, shape, and texture are each a property. (E7)

recycle [rē•sī′kəl] To use old materials to make new things. You can recycle metal, plastic, and paper to make other things. (B47)

R

rain forest [rān fôr′ist] An environment where rain falls almost every day. Many kinds of plants live in a rain forest. (B11)

reptile [rep′təl] An animal that has rough, dry skin. Snakes and lizards are each a kind of reptile. (A27)

resource [rē′sôrs′] Anything that people can use. People use resources for food and shelter. (C7)

rock [rok] A hard, nonliving thing that comes from the Earth. People use rocks to build roads and buildings. (C5)

reuse [rē′yo͞oz′] To use again. You can reuse a water bottle as a vase. (B47)

rotation [rō•tā′shən] The spinning of Earth. One complete rotation of Earth takes about 24 hours. (D8)

S

reversible [ri•vûr′sə•bəl] Able to be changed. The freezing of water to form ice is reversible. (E43)

saliva [sə•lī′və] The liquid in your mouth that begins to break down food. Food mixes with saliva when you chew. (A62)

R36

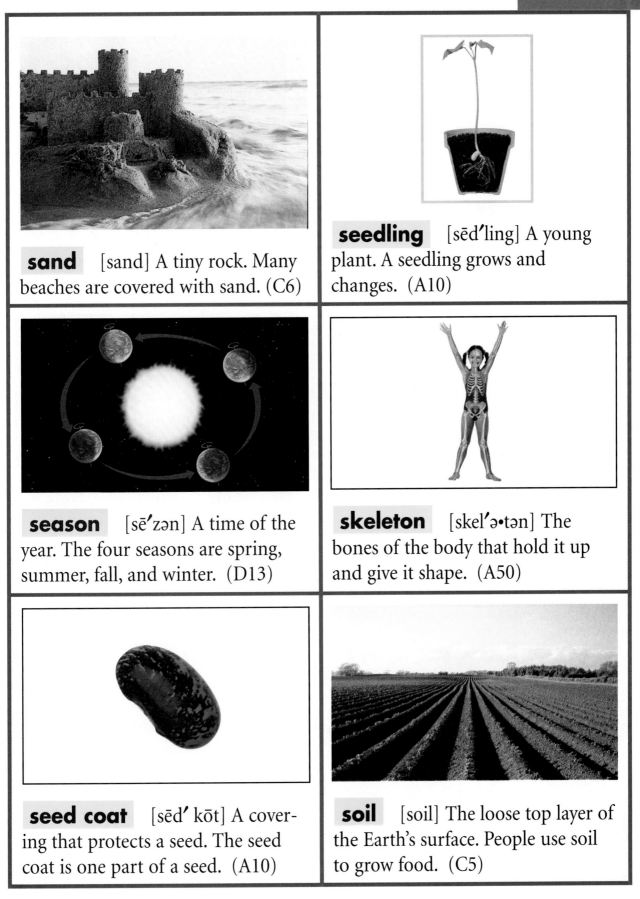

sand   [sand] A tiny rock. Many beaches are covered with sand. (C6)

seedling   [sēd′ling] A young plant. A seedling grows and changes. (A10)

season   [sē′zən] A time of the year. The four seasons are spring, summer, fall, and winter. (D13)

skeleton   [skel′ə•tən] The bones of the body that hold it up and give it shape. (A50)

seed coat   [sēd′ kōt] A covering that protects a seed. The seed coat is one part of a seed. (A10)

soil   [soil] The loose top layer of the Earth's surface. People use soil to grow food. (C5)

solar energy [sō′lər en′ər•jē]
Light and heat from the sun.
Living things on Earth are warmed
by solar energy. (D7)

sound [sound] Energy that you
hear. A sound can be loud or soft.
(F23)

solid [säl′id] The only form of
matter that has a shape of its own.
Books, furniture, and cars are each a
solid. (E9)

stomach [stum′ək] A body
part made of muscles that squeeze
food and mix it with special juices.
(A63)

sonar [sō′när′] A way to use
sounds to locate objects underwater.
Dolphins use a natural sonar by listening to echoes. (F36)

stratus [strat′əs] A kind of
cloud that is low and gray and
stretches across the sky. Stratus
clouds can bring rain. (D48)

sun [sun] The star closest to Earth. The sun is much larger than it looks from Earth. (D6)

transportation
[trans′pər•tā′shən] Ways to move people or things. Ships, cars, and airplanes are kinds of transportation. (C13)

T

temperature
[tem′pər•ə•chər]
How hot or cold something is. In summer the temperature of the air is higher than in winter. (D46)

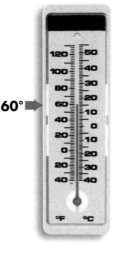

60°

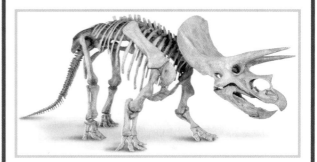

Triceratops [trī•ser′ə•täps′] A kind of dinosaur that had three horns on its head. Triceratops was a plant eater. (C38)

thermometer
[thər•mäm′ət•ər] A tool that measures temperature. Use a thermometer to measure air temperature. (D46)

V

vibrate [vī′brāt′] To move back and forth very fast. The strings of a guitar vibrate when you pluck them. (F23)

R39

water cycle   [wô′tər sī′kəl]
The way water moves from the air to the land and back to the air. (D41)

wind   [wind] The force of moving air. Wind can move sailboats, kites, pinwheels, and wind vanes. (F8)

water vapor   [wô′tər vā′pər] Water that has changed into a gas. When water is heated enough, it becomes water vapor. (D42)

woodland forest
[wood′lənd fôr′ist] An environment that gets enough rain and warmth for many trees to grow. (B12)

weather   [weth′ər] What the air is like outside. The weather is often sunny and hot in summer. (D35)

Photography Credits

Page placement key: (t) top, (c) center, (b) bottom, (l) left, (r) right, (bg) background, (i) inset

UNIT A
A02-03: Ken Biggs/Tony Stone Images; A03: Connie Hansen/The Stock Market; A06(b): Tim Davis/Photo Researchers, Inc.; A06(t): John D. Cunningham/Visuals Unlimited; A12: Grant Heilman Photography, Inc.; A13(b): David R. Frazier ; A13(t): Cathlyn Melloan/Tony Stone Images; A15(b): Morey K. Milbradt/Panoramic Images; A15(m): Gary Irving/Panoramic Images; A15(t): David Lawrence/Panoramic Images; A16(b): Runk/Schoenberger/Grant Heilman Photography, Inc.; A16(m): Michael Groen Photography; A16(mb): Superstock; A16(mt): Dr. Wm. M. Harlow/Photo Researchers, Inc.; A16(t): Doug Sokell/Tom Stack & Associates; A17(c): Superstock; A17(l): Gene Ahrens/Bruce Coleman Inc.; A17(r): Doug Sokell/Tom Stack & Associates; A18(b): G. I. Bernard/Animals Animals/ Earth Scenes; A18(m): J.C. Carton/Bruce Coleman Inc.; A18(t): Danilo Donadoni/Bruce Coleman Inc.; A20(c): John D. Cunningham/Visuals Unlimited; A20(l): Jeff Foott/DRK Photo; A20(r): Wayne Lankinen/DRK Photo; A21: Michael Groen Photography; A22-23: Flip Nicklin/Minden Pictures; A23: Richard R. Hansen/Photo Researchers, Inc.; A25(b): John E. Swedberg/Bruce Coleman Inc.; A25(mb): Mark Wagoner/Gamma-Liaison International; A25(mt): Tom Vezo/The Wildlife Collection; A25(r): Peter Davey/Bruce Coleman Inc.; A25(t): S. J. Krasemann/Photo Researchers, Inc.; A26(b): Wayne Lankinen/DRK Photo; A26(t): G. Robert Bishop/Tony Stone Images; A27(b): Denise Tackett/Tom Stack & Associates; A27(m): Michael Fogden/DRK Photo; A27(t): Renee Lynn/Tony Stone Images; A28(b): J. Carmichael/Bruce Coleman Inc.; A28(t): Marty Cordano/DRK Photo; A29(l): Brian Parker/Tom Stack & Associates; A29(r): Rex Ziak/Tony Stone Images; A31(b): S.J. Krasemann/Peter Arnold, Inc.; A31(t): Mark Newman/Bruce Coleman Inc.; A32(b): William H. Mullins/Photo Researchers, Inc.; A32(t): Tim Davis/Photo Researchers, Inc.; A33(b): Jennifer Loomis/Animals Animals/Earth Scenes; A33(m): Michael Habicht/Animals Animals/Earth Scenes; A33(t): Arthur C. Twomey/Photo Researchers, Inc.; A34: Jane Burton/Bruce Coleman Inc.; A35(l): Jane Burton/AG Stock USA; A36: David M. Dennis/Tom Stack & Associates; A37(c): Patricia Doyle/Tony Stone Images; A37(l): Renee Lynn/Tony Stone Images; A37(r): Breck P. Kent/Animals Animals/Earth Scenes; A37(t): Lemoine Jacana/Photo Researchers, Inc.; A38: Kathi Lamm/Tony Stone Images; A39(l): Ed Reschke/Peter Arnold, Inc.; A39(ml): Rod Planck/Photo Researchers, Inc.; A39(mr): Jeff Foot/DRK Photo; A39(r): D. Cavagnaro/DRK Photo; A40-41: Index Stock Photography, Inc.; A43(frames): Michael Groen Photography; A43(l): Mary T. Murphy; A43(r): Mary Kay Taylor; A44-45: Stephen Ogilvy/Picture It; A46: Paul Avis/Gamma-Liaison International; A47(t): Steve Dunwell/Image Bank; A49-52(l): Stephen Ogilvy/Picture It; A52(r)-53(l): David Madison /Bruce Coleman Inc.; A53: S. Villeger/Photo Researchers, Inc.; A55-57: Stephen Ogilvy/Picture It; A59: Tom Dee Ann Mccarthy/The Stock Market; A61-63: Stephen Ogilvy/Picture It; A64: Richard Hutchings/Picture It; A66: Mehau Kulyk/Science photo Library/Photo Researchers, Inc.; A68: Stephen Ogilvy/Picture It

UNIT B
B02-03: Frans Lanting/Minden Pictures; B05: Kim Heacox /DRK Photo; B06(b): Stephen J. Krasemann/DRK Photo; B06(m): Bill Bachmann/Stock Boston; B06(t): Bill Beatty/Visuals Unlimited; B07(b): Martin Harvey/The Wildlife Collection; B07(m): Jeff Foott/Bruce Coleman Inc.; B07(t): Ken W. Davis/Tom Stack & Associates; B09(bl): Carr Clifton/Minden Pictures; B09(br): Wayne Lynch/DRK Photo; B09(tl): Larry Ulrich/DRK Photo; B09(tr): Doug Wechsler/Animals Animals/Earth Scenes; B10(b): Joe McDonald/DRK Photo; B10(m): Larry Ulrich/DRK Photo; B10(t): Craig K. Lorenz/Photo Researchers, Inc.; B11(b): Dr. Paul A. Zahl/Photo Researchers, Inc.; B11(bkgrd): Doug Wechsler/Animals Animals/Earth Scenes; B11(m): N. H. Cheatham/DRK Photo; B11(t): Joe McDonald/Animals Animals/Earth Scenes; B12(b): Art Wolfe/Tony Stone Images; B12(m): S. Nielsen/DRK Photo; B12(t): Carr Clifton/Minden Pictures; B13(l): Wayne Lynch/DRK Photo; B13(r): Johnny Johnson/Animals Animals/Earth Scenes; B15(b): Valorie Hodgson/Visuals Unlimited; B15(t): David Sieren/Visuals Unlimited; B16(b)-17(b): Doug Sokell/Visuals Unlimited; B16(m): Tom Brakefield/Bruce Coleman Inc.; B16(t): Tim Fitzharris/Minden Pictures; B17(t): Kjell B. Sandved/Visuals Unlimited; B18(b): Flip Nicklin/Minden Pictures; B18(t)-19(l): M.C. Chamberlain/DRK Photo; B19(c): Bruce Coleman Inc.; B19(r): Flip Schulke/Black Star; B21: Bruce Gaylord/Visuals Unlimited; B22(b)-23(b): Paul Mozell/Stock Boston; B22(m): Arthur Morris/Visuals Unlimited; B22(t): Frans Lanting/Minden Pictures; B23(t): Gregory K. Scott/Photo Researchers, Inc.; B26(m): S.L. Pimm/Visuals Unlimited; B26(t): Larry Ulrich/DRK Photo; B27(m): Tom Lewis/; B28(bl): Doug Wechsler/Animals Animals/Earth Scenes; B28(br): Larry Ulrich/DRK Photo; B28(mc): Scott Nielsen/Bruce Coleman Inc.; B28(ml): David Sieren/Visuals Unlimited; B28(mr): Wayne Lynch/DRK Photo; B29: Stephen Ogilvy/Picture It; B31: Roy Morsch/The Stock Market; B33: John Eastcott/Yva Momatiuk/Stock Boston; B34(b): Joe Fuste Raga/The Stock Market; B34(t): James Burger/Bruce Coleman Inc.; B35(l): Charlie Palek/Animals Animals/Earth Scenes; B35(r): Vince Streano/The Stock Market; B36(b): John M. Roberts/The Stock Market; B36(t): Thomas Ives/The Stock Market; B37(b): Jim Steinberg/Photo Researchers, Inc.; B39: Peter Cade/Tony Stone Images; B40(b)-41(b): Stephen J. Krasemann/DRK Photo; B40(t): Tony Freeman/Photo Edit; B41(m): Robert Frerck/Odyssey Productions; B41(t): Russell D. Curtis/Photo Researchers, Inc.; B42: Wendell Metzen/Bruce Coleman Inc.; B43: Fred Bavendam/Peter Arnold, Inc.; B45: Laima Druskis/Photo Researchers, Inc.; B46: Renee Lynn/Photo Researchers, Inc.; B47(r): Bernd Wittich/Visuals Unlimited; B48: Richard Hutchings/Picture It; B49: Kelly James; B50(t): Andrew Rakoczy/Bruce Coleman Inc.; B51(t): Grant Heilman/Grant Heilman Photography, Inc.; B52(1): Robert Frerck/Odyssey Productions; B52(2): John M. Roberts/The Stock Market; B52(3): Laima Druskis/Photo Researchers, Inc.; B52(4): John Eastcott/Yva Momatiuk/Stock Boston; B52(a): Jim Corwin/Tony Stone Images; B52(b): Brian Parker/Tom Stack & Associates; B52(c): Michael Groen Photography; B52(d): B. Daemmrich/Image Works; B53(l): James Burger/Bruce Coleman Inc.; B53(r): Joe Fuste Raga/The Stock Market

UNIT C
C02-03: David Ball/The Stock Market; C03: Richard Megna/Fundamental Photographs; C05: Lee Foster/Bruce Coleman Inc.; C06(b): Michael Groen Photography; C06(t)-07(t): Tom Bean/Tom Bean Photography; C07(b): David Ball/The Stock Market; C07(mb): N.P. Alexander/Visuals Unlimited; C07(mt): Michael Groen Photography; C08(t)-09(t): Uniphoto; C09(b): Bill Everitt/Tom Stack & Associates; C11(bl): Alese/Mort Pechter/The Stock Market; C11(r): Stephen Ogilvy/Picture It; C11(tl): Uniphoto; C12(b): David Madison/Tony Stone Images; C12(m): Tom, Dee Ann McCarthy/The Stock Market; C12(t): Stephen Ogilvy/Picture It; C13(b): Jeff Greenberg/Photo Edit; C13(t): Seth Goltzer/The Stock Market; C16(b): Michael Groen Photography; C16(t): Michael Lisnet/Gamma-Liaison International; C17(b): Stephen Ogilvy/Picture It; C17(mb,mt): Michael Groen Photography; C17(t): Jonathan Rehg/Gamma-Liaison International; C18(bl): A.W. Ambler/Photo Researchers, Inc.; C18(br): Smith & Hawken; C18(ml): Biophoto Associates/Photo Researchers, Inc.; C18(mr): Michael Groen Photography; C18(tl): Chris D. Winters/Photo Researchers, Inc.; C19: Richard Hutching /Photo Edit; C20(b): Michael Groen Photography; C20(mc): Stephen Frisch/Stock Boston; C20(ml): Ed Malitsky/Gamma-Liaison International; C20(mr): David Madison/Tony Stone Images; C20(t): Lawrence Migdale/Stock Boston; C21(t): Tomas Muscionico/Contact Press Images; C21(m): Tim Thayer/Gagosian Gallery; C22(bl): Michael Groen Photography; C22(br): Dick Spahr/Gamma-Liaison International; C22(ml): Tom Bean/Tom Bean Photography; C22(mr): Debra Ferguson/AG Stock USA; C23(t): Stephen Ogilvy/Picture It; C26-C27: Tom McHugh/Photo Researchers, Inc.; C27: John Cancalosi/Peter Arnold, Inc.; C28-29: John Cancalosi/Peter Arnold, Inc.; C29(br): R.T. Nowitz/R.T. Nowitz Photos; C30(b): John Cancalosi/Stock Boston; C30(m): David Schwimmer/Bruce Coleman Inc.; C30(t): David J. Sams/Tony Stone Images; C31(b): Peter Menzel /Stock Boston; C31(m): Earl Scott/Photo Researchers, Inc.; C31(t): E.R. Degginger/Bruce Coleman Inc.; C33: Les Stone/Sygma; C34(l): David R. Frazier/Photo Researchers, Inc.; C34(r): Rich Frishman/Tony Stone Images; C35(b): Patrick Aventurier/Gamma-Liaison International; C35(t): D.B. Dutheil/Sygma; C37: Mark Perlstein/Black Star; C38-39(b): C. Chesek & D. Finnin/American Museum of Natural History; C39(t): the Royal Tyrrell Museum Library; C40(bl): A.J. Copley/Visuals Unlimited; C40: Bruce Selyem Photo /Museum of the Rockies; C41(b): Linda J. Moore */Linda J. Moore; C41(t): Francois Gohier/Photo Researchers, Inc.; C43(b): Stephen Ogilvy/Picture It; C43(t)-44: Louis Psihoyos/Matrix; C45: David M. Dennis/Tom Stack & Associates

UNIT D
D02-03: NASA/TSM/The Stock Market; D03: Uniphoto; D05: C.C. Lockwood/Animals Animals/Earth Scenes; D06-07(b): Ron Dahlquist/Tony Stone Images; D07(m): Clyde H. Smith/Peter Arnold, Inc.; D07(t): NASA/Science Source/Photo Researchers, Inc.; D08-09: Michelle Bridwell/Photo Edit; D14-15: Mug Shots/The Stock Market; D17: Scott Nielsen/Bruce Coleman Inc.; D18-19(bkgrnd): Dan McCoy/The Stock Market; D19: NASA/Peter Arnold, Inc.; D20-21: John Sanford/Science Photo Library/Photo Researchers, Inc.; D23(bkgrnd): Jeff Adamo/The Stock Market; D23(fgrnd): Stephen Frisch/Stock Boston; D24(b): Richard j. Wainscoat/Peter Arnold, Inc.; D24(t)-25(tl): Jerry Schad/Photo Researchers, Inc.; D25(b): Stephen Ogilvy/Picture It; D25(tr): John Stanford/Science Photo Library/Photo Researchers, Inc.; D26: Jerry Schad/Photo Researchers, Inc.; D27: John Sanford/Photo Researchers, Inc.; D29 & D30(5): Jerry Schad/Photo Researchers, Inc.; Jerry Schad/CREDIT; D30(5): CREDIT; D30(t): John Sanford/Science Photo Library/Photo Researchers, Inc.; D32-33: Daniele Pellegrini/Photo Researchers, Inc.; D33: Tui de Roy/Minden Pictures; D35(b): Mulvehill/Image Works; D35(t): B. Yarvin/Image Works; D36(b): Myrleen Cate/Tony Stone Images; D36(t): Mark S. Skalny/Visuals Unlimited; D37(b): Michael Black/Bruce Coleman Inc.; D37(t): W. Scarberry/Image Works; D38(b): Momatiuk/Eastcott/Image Works; D38(t): Charles Feil/Stock Boston; D39(l): David R. Frazier ; D39(r): Lawrence Migdale/Photo Researchers, Inc.; D41: Martin Bond/Science Photo Library /Photo Researchers, Inc.; D45: Cape Grim B.A.P.S./Simon Fraser/Science Photo Library/Photo Researchers, Inc.; D46(l,c): Michael Groen Photography; D46(r)-47(l): Stuart Craig, Jr./Bruce Coleman Inc.; D47(r): David Parker/Science Photo Library/Photo Researchers, Inc.; D47(t): Richard Hutchings/Picture It; D48(b): Trevor Mein/Tony Stone Images; D48(m)-49(m): John Shaw/Bruce Coleman Inc.; D48(t): Joyce Photographics/Photo Researchers, Inc.; D48(c)-D49(t): David Woods/The Stock Market; D50(b): Michael Groen Photography; D50(t): Mark Perlstein/Black Star; D51(t): Jean F. Stoick/Peter Arnold, Inc.; D52(c): Stuart Craig, Jr./Bruce Coleman Inc.; D52(l): Charles Feil/Stock Boston; D52(r): Trevor Mein/Tony Stone Images

UNIT E
E02-03: G. Brad Lewis/Gamma-Liaison International; E05: Stephen Ogilvy/Picture It; E06: Michael Groen Photography; E06(tl)-07: Stephen Ogilvy/Picture It; E09: Richard Hutchings/Picture It; E10-11: Michael Groen Photography; E12-13(r): Stephen Ogilvy/Picture It; E16-17: Michael Groen Photography; E18-19: Stephen Ogilvy/Picture It; E21: Joseph Sohm/The Stock Market; E22(l): Pat Lanza/Bruce Coleman Inc.; E22(r): Stephen Ogilvy/Picture It; E23(br): Richard Hutchings/Photo Researchers, Inc.; E23(m): Richard Hutchings/Picture It; E23(t): Royce Bair/Uniphoto; E24-25(l): Stephen Ogilvy/Picture It; E25(rb): Michael Groen Photography; E25(rt): U.S. Dept. of Transportation; E27(t): Michael Groen Photography; E28(tl,tc,4,5,6,7): Michael Groen Photography; E28(tr,2,3)-29: Stephen Ogilvy/Picture It; E30-31: Scott T. Smith/The Stock Solution; E31: Arlene L. Parnes/Photo Researchers, Inc.; E32-33: Bryan F. Peterson/The Stock Market; E33: Michael Groen Photography; E34-37: Michael Groen Photography; E39: Giovanni Simeone/The Stock Market; E42(b): Bob Lewellyn/Uniphoto; E42(t): S. Dooley/Gamma-Liaison International; E43(b): Michael Deyoung/Uniphoto; E43(t): W. A. Banaszewski/Visuals Unlimited; E45: Michael Groen Photography; E46: Stephen Ogilvy/Picture It; E46(b): Michael Groen Photography; E47: Stephen Ogilvy/Picture It; E48: Barbara Leslie/FPG International; E49: Michael Groen Photography; E51(t): Martha Cooper/Peter Arnold, Inc.; E52(b): George Mattei/Envision; E52(c): Michael Groen Photography; E52(tc): Aaron Haupt/Stock Boston; E52(tl): Michael Groen Photography; E52(tr): Barbara Leslie/FPG International

UNIT F
F02-03: Laguna Photo/Gamma-Liaison International; F03: Brian Parker/Tom Stack & Associates; F06(bl): Stephen Ogilvy/Picture It; F06(tl): David R. Frazier/Photo Researchers, Inc.; F07(t): Stephen Ogilvy/Picture It; F08(b): Richard Pasley/Stock Boston; F08(t): Don Kreuter/Rainbow; F09(b): Stephen Ogilvy/Picture It; F09(t): MacDonald Photography/Unicorn Stock Photos; F11: Frank Pennington/Unicorn Stock Photos; F12(tr): Richard Pasley/Stock Boston; F12-13(b): Richard Hutchings/Picture It; F14(b): Jim Cummins/FPG International; F18(a): B. Daemmrich/Image Works; F18(b): Jim Cummins/FPG International; F18(bottom): MacDonald Photography/Unicorn Stock Photos; F18(c): Richard Hutchings/Picture It; F18(e): Frank Pennington/Unicorn Stock Photos; F20-21: Tim Davis/Tony Stone Images; F21: Robert P. Carr/Bruce Coleman Inc.; F23: A. Ramey/Photo Edit; F24(r): Richard Hutchings/Photo Edit; F25(b): Spencer Grant/Photo Edit; F25(t): Michael Groen Photography; F26-27(l): Stephen Ogilvy/Picture It; F29: Ken Graham/Bruce Coleman Inc.; F30: Stephen Ogilvy/Picture It; F31(b): Stephen J. Krasemann/DRK Photo; F31(t): Barbara Gerlach/DRK Photo; F33: Stacy Pick/Stock Boston; F34(lt): Stephen Ogilvy/Picture It; F36: Stuart Westmorland/Tony Stone Images; F36-37: Amos Nachoum/The Stock Market; F39: Eric Freedman/Bruce Coleman Inc.; F43(cl): Spencer Grant/Photo Edit; F43(r): Doug Martin/Photo Researchers, Inc.; F44(2): A. Ramey/Photo Edit; F44(3l): Renee Lynn/Photo Researchers, Inc.; F44(3r): Robert Haddock/Tony Stone Images; F44(a): Stephen J. Krasemann/DRK Photo; F44(b): Stuart Westmorland/Tony Stone Images

All other photographs by Harcourt photographers listed below, © Harcourt:
Weronica Ankarom, Bartlett Digital Photography, Victoria Bowen, Eric Camdem, Digital Imaging Group, Charles Hodges, Ken Karp, Ken Kinzie, Ed McDonald, Sheri O'Neal, Terry Sinclair

Illustration Credits
Kate Sweeney A49, A50, A51, A52, A55, A56, A57, A58, A61, A62, A63; Steven Stankiewicz A68; Corbert Gauthier B24-25; Patrick Gnan B28; Malcolm Ellis C25; Susan Carlson C28-29; Margarita Cruz C38-39; Jon Weiman C42; Sue Carlson C44; Wendy Smith C45; Christer Eriksson D8, D9, D11, D12-13, D14- D15; Rachel Geswaldo (electronic art) D28; Tim Haggerty E2; Lori Anzalone E40; Gary Ciccarelli E41; Rachel Geswaldo (electronic art) F7; Kate Sweeney F26.